out of the clay

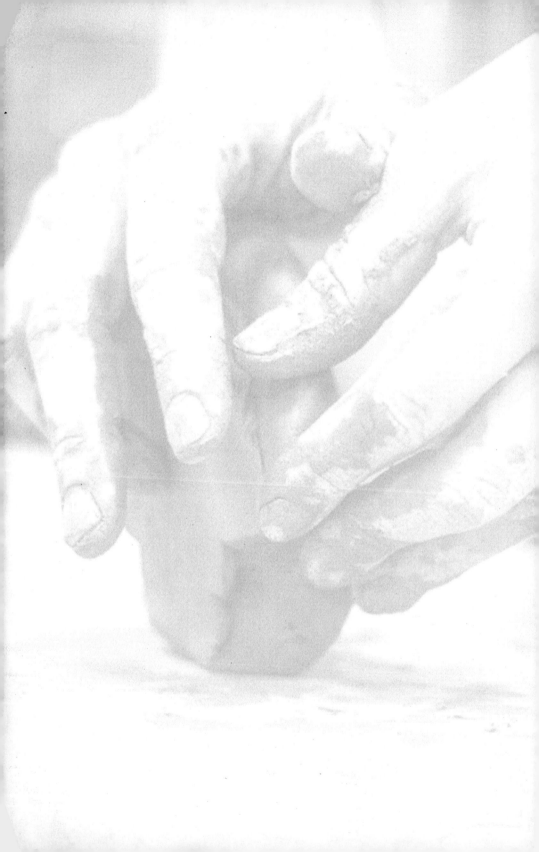

out
of
the
clay

Molding a New Generation
of Passionate Public Leaders

WILLIAM F. O'CONNOR III

BOOKLOGIX®
Alpharetta, GA

The author has tried to recreate events, locations, and conversations from his memories of them. The author has made every effort to give credit to the source of any images, quotes, or other material contained within and obtain permissions when feasible.

Copyright © 2018 by William F. O'Connor III

All rights reserved. No part of this book may be reproduced or transmitted in any form or by any means, electronic or mechanical, including photocopying, recording, or any information storage and retrieval system, without permission in writing from the publisher. For more information, address BookLogix, c/o Permissions Department, 1264 Old Alpharetta Rd., Alpharetta, GA 30005.

ISBN: 978-1-63183-357-1
eISBN: 978-1-63183-358-8
eISBN: 978-1-63183-359-5

Library of Congress Control Number: 2018910155

Printed in the United States of America   0 8 3 1 1 8

☉This paper meets the requirements of ANSI/NISO Z39.48-1992 (Permanence of Paper)

To Anne: my wife, my soul mate, my best friend. Were it not for her lifelong support, sacrifice, encouragement, vision, guidance, and love, I could have never embraced the leadership opportunities that came my way.

Success is the certain knowledge that you have become yourself, the person you were meant to be from all time.

—Dr. George A. Sheehan

Contents

Foreword		*xiii*
Preface		*xv*
PART I — MY STORY		1
1	Out of the Clay	3
2	Courageous Conversations	7
3	Dirty Socks	11
4	A Parking Problem	17
5	Dear Mame	21
6	A Fork in the Road	25
7	The Holy Grail	29
PART II — RESPECT		35
8	The Dinner Table	37
9	Mamma Cried	43
10	Essere Humano	49

11	A Picture's Worth a Thousand Words	55
12	Search? What Search?	61
13	Get a Handle on It!	67
14	All about the Buzz	73
15	Mountains out of Molehills	79
16	The Damn Dog!	85

PART III — VISION — 89

17	The Jungle	91
18	The Worst of Times	97
19	The Whole Patient	103
20	The Draft	111
21	If It Ain't Broke…	119
22	Four-Minute Mile	125

PART IV — COURAGE — 129

23	I Can't Do That!	131
24	Stop the Car!	135
25	Can You Handle the Truth?	141
26	Butter Bars	147
27	Changing a Lightbulb	153
28	What about the Bricks?	159

Part V — Intuition   167

29	Take a Seat!	169
30	Overdressed for Success	173
31	Listen to the Hum	177
32	Best Battle Ever Lost	183
33	Who, Me?	189
34	More Forks in the Road	197

Part VI — Credibility   203

35	Ahead of My Time	205
36	Doctor George	211
37	Junk in the Trunk	217
38	Back at the Dinner Table	221
39	Multiple Choice	227

Part VII — Final Thoughts   229

| 40 | The Pond | 231 |
| 41 | The Tree | 237 |

Acknowledgments   239

Foreword

by Ron Wallace
President UPS International (Ret.)
Chair of Thirty Boards around the World

Author William F. O'Connor III says it the way it is. He offers deep insights that will change the way people think about their role in public service.

O'Connor reflects on his humble beginnings and the lessons he learned while advancing through the ranks in a variety of executive-level assignments. His approach to transformational leadership is focused on people. He suggests many different ways that cause leaders to succeed, but none more important than a strong focus on appreciation and respect regardless of their position.

On the other side, he doesn't hesitate to call BS when processes, procedures, and policies simply don't work. In fact, he hits the "one way fits all, it's always been done that way" bureaucracy right between the eyes.

His success was caused by his passion for people and doing things right. He explains how he threw out the obstacles so evident in many government offices by inspiring people to be the best they can be. As he points out, efficiency matters.

Out of the Clay

His vast experience in the public sector caused him to shatter the status quo with what he often refers to as transformational leadership. O'Connor offers a road map for those willing to do the hard work and who aspire to get ahead. He wants people to be rewarded for their results, not just time in grade.

Who the heck takes on government bureaucracy? O'Connor does and pulls no punches in doing so. He gets up close and personal with leaders who have no clue on how to lead. He is not satisfied with executives who just turn the crank from day to day, producing the same old mediocre results.

He was not an office dweller. He practices and preaches a "hands-on" approach and never hesitated to get in the trenches with his people. In fact, it was a big part of his daily routine.

This book has many nuggets of wisdom as he talks about lessons learned from countless successful leaders with whom he worked. He goes into great detail on what they did that made them successful. He also talks about ineffective leaders and what they did wrong that he encountered along his long journey.

Out of the Clay is not a textbook based on research. The author simply shares his experiences to help others see a better way to perform their work. He states, "Vision is needed before transformation can be accomplished, and creating and communicating such a vision is what transformational leaders do."

This book is a must-read for anyone in, or aspiring to, a position of leadership in the public sector.

Preface

Something has got to change! And maybe, just maybe, your generation, equipped with high ideals and the passion to pursue them, can get the job done.

Face it, working in government can be a nightmare! Over the course of my long career in public service at the state, county, and local levels, I think I've pretty much seen it all. Those of you who are inside the bureaucracy have probably seen your share of it as well—painful inefficiency and ineffectiveness, dead wood, archaic one-size-fits-all policies and procedures, lack of accountability, poor morale, low productivity, lack of training, outdated technology, unfair promotion practices, ineffective management, and insufficient staffing—to name a few. I could go on, and I'll bet you could too.

Of course there are exceptions. But all too often, public servants find themselves trapped in just such a dysfunctional environment, which can easily give way to a feeling of frustration, disillusionment, cynicism, and maybe even hopelessness. As one boring day follows another, you sometimes wonder how you got there and whether your career has any purpose at all.

Out of the Clay

But it doesn't have to be that way! The antidote for all this lies in one simple word: LEADERSHIP.

I have seen firsthand the countless legions of good, hardworking, dedicated public servants who populate our organizations. I have seen struggling, frustrated people who long to do a good job, people who thirst for purpose and meaning in their work and their lives. But all too often, these good people are stuck in a bad system, not of their own making, as victims of a leadership void.

At its root, public service is all about people! In the broadest sense, it's a process of providing for the health, safety, and welfare of our people and our communities in many and varied ways. Ultimately, it's about perpetuating our society and enhancing our very quality of life. This makes public service itself both meaningful and honorable, affording a career in which one should be able to take pride in both personal contributions and organizational achievements.

But public leadership, that's a calling even more special, one that offers an incredible opportunity to significantly shape the future and make a marked difference in the lives of many. And when the public leader becomes a passionate and courageous visionary who can inspire followers and guide the ship of state into uncharted waters, new heights can be reached and profound change can emerge. Such transformational leaders answer the highest of callings in public service and are, indeed, a cut above the rest!

My guess is that you have made the same observations about dysfunctional government and want to change it. Regardless of how you have found your way into public service, by choice or by chance, you have now come to understand this leadership void and want to do something about it. You know in your heart that things can be better, both for those served by our public institutions and for those serving in them. You aspire to be one of those special leaders whose contributions are singular and lasting, a leader who makes a difference for your organization, for your people, and for our society. If that's truly the case, I can help you!

However, let me be clear. If efficient "public administration" is your only interest—a career of organizing, supervising, tracking, measuring, and reporting—don't bother to read any further. If you will be satisfied with being a milquetoast manager who simply makes sure your people show up when they are supposed to and put the right papers in the right box, just gently place this book "back on the shelf."

But if it's change you want to achieve—significant, dynamic, bone-crunching, transformative change through leadership—then this is the book for you! If you want to transform archaic, inflexible, unresponsive, rule-driven, one-size-fits-all bureaucracies into high-performing, results-oriented, flexible, customer-focused models of good government, a role where you are a cynicism buster who restores faith in our public institutions, then please read on.

Now, I know that sounds all well and good, but transformation in government is not easily achieved. As I will discuss at length, the public sector is a unique animal with its own set of characteristics and problems. Public leaders must deal with many challenges and limitations not faced by their private-sector counterparts. That doesn't mean that transformation in the public sector is not possible. It just means it takes a special brand of leader to do it.

You may think that you are just an ordinary person not capable of such transformational leadership, not wealthy, not Ivy League, not born into a leadership legacy. Or maybe your career to date has gone in a different direction, and you just suddenly and unexpectedly landed in government. Public service wasn't part of your plan.

I need to tell you that I am just such an ordinary person who grew up in a working-class, blue-collar family in rural Upstate New York. I wanted to be an architect, but somehow I just "woke up" one day and found myself in government, and I didn't like it. I didn't like it at all! After many failed attempts to escape the bureaucracy, I eventually grew to understand and embrace public service and learned that organizations could be changed dramatically through leadership. I came to see public leadership as the high calling to which I alluded earlier and a wonderful way to make a meaningful contribution to our way of life.

More than that, I learned that such transformational leadership can result in a career that is fulfilling and rewarding beyond belief, a way to put purpose and passion in your life and meet that highest of human needs: leaving a legacy. Except for my family and my faith, it has been this opportunity to lead and drive transformative change that I value above all.

I only wish I had this book to read when I was getting started in my public career, as I could have made a difference much sooner and done it much better. My goal here is to share what I've learned with you so that you can make a difference much sooner, and do it much better!

Now, I need to tell you that this is not a textbook. It's not based on years of research or academic study, and it won't tell you exactly what to do or how to do it. There are no methods, tools, or techniques presented here. For that I direct your attention to the wealth of management and leadership literature written by expert scientists and thought leaders in the field. Throughout my career, this body of work helped me find my way, and I am certain it will help you.

In contrast, this book is a collection of short stories that I hope you will find entertaining, thought-provoking, and maybe even inspiring. The stories that I share with you are taken from my own life and work and are reflections on the leadership and life lessons of my personal experience and observations. Rather than showing you "what to do," these stories are intended to show you "what to be" as a person and as a leader.

It is through these years of experience and observation that I have concluded that there are five distinct personal attributes that define transformational leaders. The attributes of respect, vision, courage, intuition, and credibility are what set these leaders apart from their brethren who simply hold down the job, put in their

Preface

time, revel in the trappings of office, and preside over the mediocrity-without-end of the status quo.

I have seen this play out in state agencies, county departments, and in the halls of local government. I have seen it in public education and in the military. I have seen it at work in small ten-person offices all the way up to ten-thousand-person departments and beyond. Time and time again, I have observed that these are the characteristics that separate those who fundamentally change the shape of government and the course of events from those timid beings who will just accept things as they find them, assuming, "It is what it is!"

Quite unconventionally, some of my leadership stories are based in childhood experiences or family life and begin in a manner that may not seem relevant. Then, other more conventional stories emanate from the world of work, as you might expect. Some stories introduce you to real friends and associates, including three special mentors who showed me that ordinary people can, in fact, achieve extraordinary things. There are stories that take lessons from fictional characters, while others introduce you to family members including my parents, my kids, my little old grandmother, crazy Aunt Ruth—and, oh yes, I can't forget the family dog.

Throughout the book, you will meet some outstanding public leaders whom I have known and worked with personally, ordinary people from humble beginnings who rose to do great things. Commissioners, college presidents, principals, superintendents, directors, and military officers, all otherwise ordinary people whom you would never hear about, who somehow drew lessons from their mentors and personal experience to become transformational leaders in government. Without knowing it, they passed these lessons on to me.

Each part of the book is developed around one of the five characteristics I mentioned above. But since life doesn't exist in wholly discrete buckets, there is overlap in almost every story where threads or hints of the other themes are evident.

Further, I ask you to stay alert as you read, as there are many "lessons learned" that wend their way through the pages, even though they may not be completely central to the theme of that particular story. Some are mini-essays on observations or conclusions on related topics or issues, while others are just "sound bites" that may stick with you long after the book is forgotten.

The fact is I've tried a lot of things over my career. Thankfully, I got some of it right, and regrettably, some of it wrong, but I learned from it all. In telling my story, I talk about things I have studied, things I have observed, things I have done, and things that have happened to me. This collection of short stories is intended to illustrate how life, if we pay attention, provides useful lessons in many different ways, some quite unexpected.

While the routes to transformation are infinite and vary from one organization to another, I am certain that the leader of such transformation must exhibit these five personal characteristics, or the transformation will fail. My goal is to help you understand and mold yourself and your leadership legacy around these essential attributes.

Each of you will have your own personal story where your life and career will play out in its own special way. My stories are intended to inspire, stimulate thought and reflection, and help you see how you might become one of those transformational public leaders we so desperately need. If you can find a way to rise to this high calling, you will make a real difference in the lives of many and, in doing so, experience the joy and satisfaction of an incredibly rewarding career.

So, drawing on these many years of public service, and as did my own mentors and role models, I want to pass on the most valuable of these lessons to you, the new generation of passionate public leaders. Everything I have, both tangible and intangible, is a result of the wonderful opportunity I have had to spend a lifetime in public service. Writing this book feels like my final responsibility.

PART I

MY STORY

Chapter 1

Out of the Clay

As I looked into their eyes, I could see the urgency, the intense fear that comes only in a life-or-death situation. I could feel the exhaustion, see the courage, and understand the sacrifice! I found myself caught in an emotional response, a tiny tear in the corner of my eye, a tingling in my spine. How could this be? It was only a block of clay!

Actually, it was a bit more than just a block of clay. It was a block of clay that had been molded into an incredible depiction of two firefighters in 1960-era turnout gear rescuing a fallen brother, dragging him away from the massive wall that would ultimately bear the names of those firefighters of New York State who had fallen in the line of duty. This was the last of four artistic proposals to be considered by the advisory committee.

I had the honor of being the facilitator on this important project and very much enjoyed working with this advisory group of top people representing the fire service in New York State, both paid and volunteer. They were focused, of a like mind, tough, decisive, and gutsy, exactly what I had expected of the leaders of this brave profession.

After the advisors selected a location for this memorial on the Empire State Plaza in Albany, the epicenter of New York State government, they set criteria for a figurative sculptural work. Their guidance was simple, clear, and direct, just as expected. Armed with these criteria, we began an open process for the selection of a sculptor. Ultimately, four artists were short-listed and paid a modest honorarium to prepare a three-dimensional proposal.

On the day of review and selection, each artist came before the panel, one after the other, clutching their proposals much like grade-school kids headed for show-and-tell. The first three submissions were excellent, and it would have been quite difficult to select one over the other.

Then, the fourth artist entered the conference room with a large maquette molded out of red clay as I described above. Far more impressive than any of the prior three, it was detailed with incredible accuracy from the hip boots, to the buckles on the rubber raincoats, to the cracks in the battle-scarred leather helmets. But the faces, oh those haunting faces! Aged beyond their years, they told an indelible story of exhaustion, fear, courage, and sacrifice.

I had never seen such a powerful and impressive piece of work. As I looked at the body language of the panel, firefighters all, my sense was that the competition was over as soon as that maquette was placed on the table.

The only thing this new artist had going against him was that he had never had a large commission, not one. Yet, as I expected they would, this panel of direct, decisive, gutsy guys relied on what their instincts told them and voted unanimously to award this young man his first major commission. So, not only did this decision result in a beautiful, moving, and singularly significant memorial for New York, it launched the career of a truly gifted young sculptor.

However, the story of cleaving, molding, and transforming a

simple block of red clay into a spectacular work of art is not the story I want to tell. The story here is really about the transformation or the molding of the artist himself, Robert Eccleston.

Robert began his career by studying industrial design in college. He graduated through the Reserve Officer Training Corps (ROTC) program and, rising to the rank of captain, spent six years as an officer in the United States Army, teaching in the Mountain Warfare School, which, he admits, he "took to like a fish to water."

But all the while, he had an incredible gift, and his destiny lay quietly hidden within. Throughout his military tour of duty, he never forgot his love for drawing and creating. He found himself sketching whenever he could. And during his fourth year of active military duty, he sensed he was being drawn in another direction and took a continuing-education course in sculpture.

This unleashed his inner passion, and his hobby quickly turned into a commitment to pursue sculpture as a profession. Over a two-year period, he was transformed from soldier to artist, and the world is better for it as he continues to transform blocks of red clay, molten bronze, and stainless steel into beautiful works of art, both nationally and internationally.

The story of Rob Eccleston's transformation has caused me to reflect on my own career and transformation, a career that began in architecture and construction, took me kicking and screaming into government, and culminated in the opportunity of a lifetime: the opportunity to lead people, the opportunity to transform organizations, and the opportunity to change lives. More importantly, it gave me the opportunity to make a difference!

How did this all happen? On the pages that follow, I reflect on how various events, people, and circumstances in my life influenced and molded me into what, I feel, I was destined to become from the very beginning.

Regardless of where your own career may have started or where it has taken you thus far, I suspect that you are beginning to see the potential rewards of public service and already aspire to a life of leadership. Your own transformation is well underway and you know now that you, too, want to make a difference. I can't help but wonder how many other potential leaders are out there with you just waiting to be drawn out of the clay.

The premise of this book is my belief that such transformations are possible, that leaders are not simply born but must be molded, just as unique pieces are molded by the sculptor. And my experience suggests that the greatest public leaders have been shaped in a way such that they uniformly exhibit the five key attributes that I present and explore on the coming pages.

As I said in the preface, my goal here is to help you come to know and understand these attributes so that you can shape yourself around them, embrace them, practice them, and have your legacy of leadership guided by them.

So, as you read my stories about what influences shaped and molded me, I ask you to reflect on your own life experiences, interests, and passions and begin to discern who and what you can ultimately become. And that out of the clay, out of the raw material that is you, may emerge a truly transformational leader.

A leader who can garner the respect needed to lead people to somewhere they have never been. A leader who can create and articulate a vision of where that new somewhere is. A leader who can muster the courage to buck the status quo and defy overwhelming odds in order to get there. A leader who can sense some things that can't be seen and skillfully employ intuition as well as data. And a leader who is believable and has compelling credibility.

My greatest hope is that, on the pages of this little book, you, and others, will hear the call to become part of a new generation of dedicated, talented, and passionate public leaders that we so desperately need to reshape, reform, reinvent, and reenergize our public institutions and restore trust and confidence in our government.

CHAPTER 2

COURAGEOUS CONVERSATIONS

The Arlington Public Schools (APS) system in Northern Virginia is rich with cultural diversity. According to their website, there are more than twenty-four thousand students from 111 different nations speaking eighty-eight different languages enrolled there. Without a doubt, this presents a unique set of circumstances for faculty and administrators.

In order to embrace this great diversity and improve its cultural competency, the system pursues a program entitled "Courageous Conversations" where administrators, supervisors, and senior staff meet several times a year in large and small group sessions to explore and share thoughts on this important topic. Discussions focus on how individual perceptions of race impact the academic, social, and emotional growth of students and the performance of staff.

The program allows students and faculty to develop positive relationships, develop skill sets to increase achievement, and come to better understand the experiences, perspectives, and contributions represented through the different cultures present in the school system. The goal is to find ways to effectively engage every student (regardless of background), prove that every child can learn, and eliminate achievement gaps.

At one of these large events, a select few leaders were asked to share their own life stories with the assembled group. As it turned out, these stories were powerful and more emotional than expected, as everyone present couldn't help but reflect on their own individual stories, how they got where they are today, the hurdles and adversity they had to overcome, and the people who helped them get there. After this, it was easier to make the bridge to the lives of their own students and sense the important roles they were playing in helping these kids write their own stories.

I was privileged to work in the APS Facilities and Operations Division at the time, and our assistant superintendent, Clarence Stukes, had been one of those leaders selected to share his story at that large event. At one of our divisional staff meetings, our group of about eight managers had the opportunity to view a videotape of his presentation. It was incredibly powerful and quite emotional as we learned how this man's life unfolded from a childhood of little hope to a highly successful professional career. He was, indeed, one of the finest public leaders I had ever met.

For this man, there were many obstacles to overcome, a few lucky breaks, some people who helped, and lots of dedication and hard work along the way. There was nothing guaranteed or certain about this, as there were many forks in the road that could have led to a completely different outcome. This presentation gave us fresh insight into who he was, and it reshaped what we thought of him and how we interacted with him.

Consequently, it was with enthusiasm that we embraced his proposal that we all share our stories with each other in a similar way. And so it began at one staff meeting per month with each of us taking a turn. This sharing was an incredibly informative and emotional experience, both for the presenter and listeners.

As we worked through the process, we began to understand and appreciate each other more and worked together with a greater sense of respect and collegiality. These were truly courageous conversations in every sense. It turned out that the stories were harder to tell than expected, and sometimes difficult to hear. We stopped seeing our colleagues simply as benign elements moving around us, but began seeing them more clearly and appreciating them as human beings. They were no longer just part of the backdrop of our own autobiographies. Indeed, these courageous conversations helped us see ourselves differently and permanently changed the tenor of the division.

In the spirit of these courageous conversations, I want to briefly share my own story with you. As I do it, I want you to see that there is nothing automatic or preordained about life. Some things work out and some things don't. But in every case, we have free will and choices to make, good and bad, all along the way. Regardless of your family origin, your gender, your race, your nationality, your socioeconomic background, your physical ability, or anything else, I am quite certain you are capable of doing great things! As you read my unlikely story, I ask you to reflect on your own story and how it has unfolded so far. I want you to see the potential you have to influence and shape your own future and, if you choose, aspire to the important role of public leadership.

Chapter 3

Dirty Socks

Have you ever noticed how the sense of smell has the potential to conjure up all manner of memory, feeling, and emotion? Apple blossoms, lilacs, fresh-cut hay—they all trigger important memories for me. But the rich aroma of the moist earth as it's turned over in spring in preparation for planting is one I still find among the most powerful. It takes me all the way back to my childhood growing up in the wide-open farm country south of Troy, New York, a small upstate city whose Civil War–era industrial prominence had long passed.

It was there, at the age of six or so, that I would follow Ed Jordan and his small, red Farmall tractor back and forth across the fields, walking right down in the furrow as the plow folded back the earth. Invariably, I would come in the house with dirt-filled shoes and socks so filthy my mother could hardly scrub them clean. "Where have you been? What have you been doing to get your socks so dirty?" my mother would ask. "Oh nothing, just helping Ed plow the field."

Reflecting on this now, it really was an unlikely beginning for what was to come, a long way from blue pinstripe suits and polished wingtips. We were a blue-collar family and didn't have much money, even though both of my parents worked. My mother had a tenth-grade education, but my father left school during the tenth grade and never went back.

In those early days, my father was a "maintenance man" in the county welfare home and my mother was an entry-level bookkeeper in a state government agency. They had built and mortgaged our little Cape Cod–style house for $3,500 just before the United States entered World War II. This modest dwelling sat on a postage-stamp lot surrounded by the Jordan farm.

To me, this was heaven and a great place to grow up. And as far as we knew as kids, we had everything we needed. We had no understanding that the garden behind the house and the vegetables my mother put up for the winter were a necessity. Sifting the ashes for "clinkers" to put back in the coal furnace, saving rags and newspapers, and even saving string from the bake-shop boxes were other memorable aspects of our household economy.

My mother sewed some of her own clothes, and for a while, we had to borrow my grandmother's car when my father couldn't afford, or find the parts, to keep his ancient 1928 Chevy running—all signs of our modest means. I remember clearly one very cold winter night when my father was breaking up some old wooden furniture to keep the fire in the boiler going because we had run out of coal. For me, that was fun!

But life was good! We didn't have video games, organized sports, or even a city park to play in, but we enjoyed the freedom of open space and the creativity of free play. We had to make our own fun, and, I guess, it frequently ended with dirty socks!

We built forts on the ground and forts in the trees. We dug tunnels and dammed the creek with logs, rocks, and mud. Riding bikes, climbing trees, playing ball in the field, or flying kites were just some of the wonderful things we did to occupy our time. In spite of parental warnings that we were going to "knock an eye out," we had a fun game of "war" in which we threw small green apples at each other while running through the woods. We had a great old red barn to climb in and a bounty of apples, peaches, cherries, pears, rhubarb, and strawberries. Yes indeed, life was good!

My parents were but a sign of things to come. Post-war America saw a wave of families abandoning city life for the lower density and fresh air of the suburbs, and our open space began to dwindle. As more people discovered the beauty and quality of life in "the country," the fields and woods where we lived and played were slowly transformed into neighborhoods of closely spaced, ranch-style, wood-and-brick boxes.

While the open space was shrinking, all of this development and construction provided us with some new ways to get our socks dirty: playing in excavations, climbing on and through the partially constructed homes, and simply watching the bulldozers move the earth or the carpenters assemble the frames. As a spin-off benefit, we had a virtually unlimited supply of scrap material for building our own forts, bridges, and tree houses.

As I got older and wanted to have some money of my own, dirty play gave way to dirty work. I had a paper route of almost one hundred customers who paid 42 cents a week for the Monday through Saturday editions of the *Troy Record*. I got to keep about 1.5 cents per paper. Rain or shine, hot or cold, I hauled the papers in a canvas sack slung over my shoulder as I rode my bike up and down the hills of my five-mile rural route. My customers thought it ingenious when I wound old clothesline rope through the spokes and around the tires of my bike to give me traction in the deep snow.

I mowed lawns and trimmed shrubbery, shoveled snow off of walks and driveways, cleaned garages and basements. After my father became a licensed electrician, I followed him around for one dollar an hour handing him tools, drilling holes, and pulling cables as he did electrical projects at night or on weekends. I was willing to take on any job, no matter how dirty or difficult, to make a buck.

I remember one particular job my father took on was the rewiring of a three-story brick house in the city that had been gutted by fire. It was very hot that summer and I would usually finish the day covered in an itchy combination of sweat, plaster dust, and ashes. Yes, even my socks were dirty! I'm sure my father was proud to see his boy unafraid to embrace difficult and dirty work and make the connection between effort and reward.

I don't know to what extent all of this building of things, things I built myself and things I watched being built, or my love of drawing led to my childhood dream of becoming an architect. While most of my family thought I would follow in my father's footsteps and become an electrician or other tradesman, all I ever remember wanting to do was to grow up to design beautiful homes, churches, and fire stations. I was not at all dissuaded by our humble beginnings or our modest financial means, or by the fact that no one in our very large extended family had ever attended college.

During career week in the seventh grade, an architect visited our class and talked about the profession. That settled it for me, and that's what I set out to do. All of my study and preparation from that point on, including getting accepted at my dream school, Rensselaer Polytechnic Institute in Troy, New York, was designed to attain this vision of becoming an architect and a well-respected member of the community. But as I learned, and you probably already know, life doesn't always work out as planned!

Again, I'm sharing my story as a means to cause you to reflect on your own story. But my main message at this point is to encourage you to not let your own humble beginnings, your own economic limitations, your own family situation, or your own "dirty socks," so to speak, hold you back or get in the way of your dreams. You are free to create your own vision and choose your own path. While life is not easy and doesn't always work out as planned, you can choose to continue to work hard, continue to prepare, and continue to seize opportunities as they will, most certainly, present themselves.

And as you attain increasingly higher office, please don't forget where you came from. The greatest role models I had in my career, some of whom you will meet later, were uniformly of very humble beginnings, and they never lost sight of that. They never forgot how they got started, the breaks they had, or the people who helped them along the way. No matter how high they rose or how much power or authority they attained, they never considered themselves superior to anyone. They never put themselves above others and regularly tapped into this humble background as an indicator of "true north," as a source of understanding, as a means to build relationships, and as the fuel for inspirational leadership.

Looked at correctly, such humble beginnings become more of an asset to the leader than a liability. Just for fun, let's think of this as "the power of the dirty socks"!

Now, back to my story . . .

CHAPTER 4

A Parking Problem

Yes, life doesn't always work out as planned!

By now, most of us have attended a commencement or two and heard a number of keynote speakers. Included among the many I have heard were some great people, such as Secretary of State Madeleine Albright and Holocaust survivor Elie Wiesel. Such personalities are always impressive, and they never fail to communicate inspiring messages. But shame on me, the messages don't stick too far beyond the commencement exercise itself. Maybe you have experienced the same thing.

In fact, I only remember one such message. It was a comment made by Dr. Andrew Bergman during his keynote address at our daughter's graduation from Binghamton University in 1994. Dr. Bergman had studied history at Binghamton and eventually became a noted screenwriter, film director, and novelist.

In the context of the Binghamton campus, Dr. Bergman said something like this: "Finding your place in life is like finding a parking space at the West Gym!" He went on to explain that you may want one near the door or you may want one under a tree, but you have to take the best one available at the time. You have to park someplace and make the best of it until you can find a space more to your liking. And so it is with a career.

I think we have all seen this or experienced it firsthand. An engineering major in my college class became a prominent television news anchor. I know a psychology major who became a consultant in homeland security, an English major who is a vice president at a four-year college, a board-certified surgeon who works in health information and management systems, and a social-work graduate who is an events planner. I even know a brilliant public leader who grew up wanting to be a marine biologist, eventually became a police officer, but today is an assistant city manager in a major metropolitan city.

It happens. It may be happening to you. You have to respond to opportunities as they present themselves, park someplace as it were, until you find something better. Very often, this initial opportunity actually leads to a long-term career. I'm sure, as a kid, you were asked, "What do you want to be when you grow up?" I doubt any of you responded, "A government bureaucrat." But I would encourage you to be open to that possibility, as the opportunity for a rewarding career may be close at hand.

As I mentioned in the last chapter, I grew up building things and drawing things with a vision of becoming an architect. When I got accepted to my dream school, I was certain that I could convert this vision into a reality.

College got off to a rough start. With two Cs, two Ds, and two Fs after the first six weeks, I feared I was about to demonstrate that my high school guidance counselor's prediction was right. She had said that even if I got accepted at Rensselaer, which she highly doubted, I probably wouldn't make it. Thank you, Martha, for the motivation to prove you wrong!

I somehow got through my freshman year with decent grades and was on the Dean's List the rest of the way. I got stronger each year as more and more of the course work was specific to the profession of architecture. Architectural design, structural engineering, building materials, mechanical equipment, and even architectural history all interested me, and I did well.

So after six years of hard work, armed with a master's degree in architecture and filled with ideals, I was ready to attack the world. I certainly hoped the profession of architecture was ready for me. Here I was, ready to fulfill that dream!

Unfortunately, I couldn't find a job with a local architectural firm, an apprenticeship to which most new graduates aspired. I became desperate and broadened my search to any position where my skills might be of use. Construction, graphics, teaching, marketing, even a printing company—nothing! I did, indeed, have a "parking problem"!

Up until that point, everything had been somewhat planned out. Now I was in uncharted waters, and the situation was dismal. Fortunately, I had a part-time instructor position teaching drafting at the community college in the evening. After class one night, I shared my plight with a few of my students who hung back to chat for a while. Two of them happened to be employed in what was known at that time as the state architect's office or, more formally, the Division of Architecture in the New York State Department of Public Works.

My students gave me the name of the principal architect, Al Brevetti. I called him the next day, was invited for an interview, and was offered a job as an entry-level junior architect. Finally, after "circling the lot" for many weeks, I had found a "parking space" and was going to be an architect at last! But . . .

CHAPTER 5

DEAR MAME

Dear Mame,

After many years alone, I recently met a wonderful young woman who just may be "the one." We have been dating for several months and I am absolutely crazy about her. I just need your advice related to my family situation. My younger brother has a steady job with the State, but my older brother, a carpenter, can't seem to hold a job due to alcoholism. My father is in Sing Sing serving five to ten years for armed robbery, and my mother is in Albany County Jail awaiting sentencing for her fourth shoplifting conviction. We're not sure where my sister is, but the last we knew she was in New York City working as a prostitute. What I want to know, Mame, is should I tell my girlfriend that my brother works for the State?

Welcome to the public sector, Mr. O'Connor!

In addition to the employee handbook, the standard procedures manual, and the state building code that were provided by management during my first days on the job, a coworker handed me a copy of this fictitious advice column. Those few words summed up quite well what I was to quickly come to understand to be the poor self-image the organization had of itself and, I might add, that the outside world had of it as well. As my first weeks unfolded, I learned why this was the case, and my first "parking space" soon became a nightmare!

Landing in state government turned out to be both frustrating and embarrassing. Nothing in six years of college study prepared me for the culture shock that I experienced as an idealistic graduate crashing headlong into a large and lethargic government bureaucracy. I was clearly viewed as a second-class citizen by my college classmates who had secured positions in private practice or academia. With a whiff of elitism, some even suggested that the time served "working for the State" wouldn't count toward the three-year apprenticeship required for taking the architectural licensing examination.

It's not that there weren't talented and hardworking professionals on the staff. There were. Plenty of them. The problem was with the organization itself. It was very large with many discrete, uncoordinated, and often feuding departments that functioned with great autonomy. Architects generally enjoyed making designs for building projects with little regard for what the client agency wanted, needed, or could afford. Schedules were routinely ignored, and some designs were prepared for buildings that were unfunded or that the client no longer needed.

There lacked a clear sense of organizational purpose and management was mostly inept, performed by architects and engineers who were very competent in their professions, but not in management. They would rather be designing and drawing and spent most of their time studying projects. Most certainly, there was no leadership.

Personnel policies were abysmal and discipline or adherence

to the rules was spotty. Great numbers of employees routinely arrived late, left early, and took extended work breaks every morning and afternoon. It seemed to me that for every one person who was working hard, there was another one milking the system. There was even a bit of dead wood not doing much at all. A little private work got done on state time and pilfering of minor items from the stock room was not uncommon.

Clearly, there was an entitlement mentality wherein there was no conscious connection between doing work and collecting a paycheck. There was an emphasis on civil-service "title" and getting promoted from one position to the next in order to achieve greater compensation. Those employees high on promotion lists kept a watchful eye on those close to retirement, or those in ill health. More than once I heard a comment like, "I can't wait until 'Joe' retires! He's got my title!"

Many people sat for any civil-service exam for which they were eligible, even if they didn't have any interest in doing that type of work. Incredibly, there was even keen competition for supervisory and management positions by people who really wanted no part of supervision or management.

There was little pride or sense of organizational identity. The greatest pride surrounded the State Architect's Bowling League and the State Architect's Retiree Club. It was there that the "old-timers" gathered for lunch on a monthly basis and relived their "glory days" of designing and building large, new mental hospitals and developing fallout shelters during the Cold War.

Leadership was so lacking, and the performance of the organization so unsteady, that it had resulted in the statutory or executive creation of other organizations, entities, or programs within government to take on significant portions of the State's program in design and construction. The state architect was perceived as not able to get the job done, evidenced by the fact that when that state architect retired, he was replaced by an administrative director. In fact, there were at least two initiatives designed to eliminate the agency completely, but both failed due to union and political pressure.

Out of the Clay

My first few weeks were so frustrating and disappointing that I contemplated quitting outright. I remember attending a briefing on employee benefits and hearing an enthusiastic presentation on the retirement system. I was told that I could collect full retirement benefits at the age of fifty-five. Yikes! I wasn't going to be there for another thirty days, much less thirty more years—or so I thought!

I cast my net for another job. I just couldn't see wasting my life in government! I wanted to do something that made a difference! I still had this notion of designing and drawing and becoming a well-respected architect.

But such a position was not to be had at that point, and after eleven months in state service, it was time for me to report for active duty with the United States Army Corps of Engineers. Having been commissioned through the ROTC program at Rensselaer, I had an obligation to serve two years.

As an instructor at the engineer school at Fort Belvoir, Virginia, and later as a construction operations officer in Vietnam, I was exposed to some exceptionally great leaders, as well as some frightfully poor leaders. I'll share lessons from both later.

Anyway, after more than two years on active duty, I returned to my position with the State of New York. My plan was to work there until I could find something better. Other than the elimination of the position of state architect, and a name change for the organization, the place was pretty much the same. In fact, I was asked to pick up and continue a research study that I had to set aside when I left twenty-seven months earlier.

However, one thing was different than before I left. I was informed by some of the old-timers that now that I was a combat veteran, I was untouchable in the civil-service system. Basically, I could do pretty much nothing for the next thirty years and still collect my full pension. Yikes!

Clearly, this was just not my idea of a meaningful career or meaningful life! The state architect and I had no future together, of that I was sure!

But as I said earlier, life doesn't always work out as planned . . .

CHAPTER 6

A Fork in the Road

Yogi Berra, the thirteen-time New York Yankees World Series Champion, is usually credited with some interesting sayings. "It ain't over till it's over." "Baseball is ninety percent mental and the other half is physical." "It's like déjà vu all over again." But one of my favorites is "When you come to a fork in the road, take it!"

Now obviously, one must go one way or the other at a fork and either direction represents a decision, a decision to be made without knowing what either path holds in store, or where either road will ultimately lead. This happens often in a career, and such decisions can have lasting impact. And so it was with the decision I was to make next.

While searching for an escape route from public service, I decided to seek a position within the organization that might be more exciting or fulfilling while I "looked around." Happily, I found a new home in the Office of Project Management, a small but highly visible office where a group of eight hand-picked project managers guided the larger, consultant-designed projects from "cradle to grave." As an added benefit, there was minimal need to interact with the vast archaic line agency that I described in the last chapter.

To prepare me for this responsibility, I was sent to New York City for a week-long training seminar on project management. It was here that I came to a fork in the road, so to speak, one that I did not anticipate. During this week, I was exposed to some exceptional professionals in the field, most of whom had been responsible for major projects in the New York City region. Included on the program was the project manager for CBS who led the 1967 modernization of the old Yankee Stadium.

The person who made the most significant impact on me, however, was a PhD who had been responsible for designing the organizational structure for NASA's Apollo space program. Although his presentation centered on Apollo, he introduced me to the concept of management as a discipline in its own right. The study of architecture included only one course on professional practice but nothing on management, organizational behavior, or leadership.

It was an epiphany of sorts! I sensed that a nerve had been touched. It suddenly and unexpectedly appeared that management and leadership held great potential for me, especially in an organization with a dearth of such things. As I looked at my organization, where all the other architects and engineers were mostly concerned with the practice of their professions, I sensed a golden opportunity here for someone who would come along with real management and leadership skills, skills the organization so sorely needed.

Just this one seminar helped me understand that my agency, with all its problems and flaws, was not terribly unique. Like so many other organizations, we had many good people, we just lacked leadership. It became obvious to me that there was a great problem to solve here, a worthy endeavor to undertake, and the possibility of a rewarding career at hand.

Consequently, I stopped looking to escape from public service!

Part I: My Story   A Fork in the Road

I enrolled in the MBA program at Rensselaer on a part-time basis with a concentration in the public sector. I had decided I would work to make a difference, one position at a time, from the bottom up. Forget about designing and drawing. I wanted to lead! I suppose this was pretty gutsy for a relatively new employee, but a passion had been ignited and I was "all in" from that point on.

Statistics almost derailed my plan right off the bat. Having been out of college for five years, I knew it was going to be difficult, especially since my math skills were a little "rusty." My advisor suggested that I take this required course first. He said that he would be teaching it (he boasted that in twenty years of teaching, no one ever got a perfect paper on any of his exams), that it was very difficult, and that if I got through it, I would probably be able to complete the forty-two-credit-hour program.

So, I registered for the course and off I went to the bookstore. In the vernacular of the current texting era, OMG! As I looked through the statistics textbook, the math may as well have been Chinese. Then it got worse! I turned out to be a novelty at my first night of classes when I showed up with a slide rule. My classmates, all recent engineering graduates, had new Texas Instruments electronic calculators. LOL!

Statistics proved to be a heavier lift than I anticipated, but I was determined to not let it derail my newly chosen career path. I worked harder than ever and pulled out a B for the class. From there on, I doubled up in classes each semester and earned an A in everything else. Finally, after three years of hard work, I received my MBA—not to mention a great feeling of self-satisfaction!

I've heard it said that "luck is when opportunity and preparation come together." Well, I was about to get lucky, moving to a better "parking space," so to speak. Just as I was completing the three-year MBA program (preparation), the competitive civil-service examination for first-line supervisor was announced (opportunity). It was an oral examination that allowed me to give management- and leadership-laden answers to relatively technical questions. The field was large, and I suspect the examination panel heard things from me that they had not heard from any of the other candidates. And maybe more importantly, they sensed my passion to take charge and to lead. The panel awarded me a perfect score, far ahead of the closest competitor, and placed me first on the promotion list.

However, getting appointed to that first supervisory position was not easy and will be discussed in a later chapter. But appointed I was. And so began an exciting and rewarding career in public leadership. From this small beginning leading twelve architects and drafting technicians, all the way through the ranks to deputy commissioner, I continually and consistently looked for ways to "blow things up" and transform whatever I was responsible for into a model of good government.

I won't take any space here, or later, giving you a blow by blow of thirty-eight-plus years of state service or the exciting leadership opportunities that would follow. I will simply tell you stories of things that happened along the way, or observations I've made, as they serve to describe the five essential attributes of the transformational public leader as I see them.

I've said it before, but I want to say it again for emphasis! For the right person, public leadership can be an incredibly rewarding career, providing an overwhelming sense of self-worth, a feeling that you accomplished something meaningful, and fulfilling that basic human need of leaving a legacy. So as Yogi Berra advises, when you come to a fork in the road, take it—especially if it might result in a leadership opportunity.

Meanwhile, keep in mind that definition of luck described above, and continually prepare yourself in whatever way you can, and as hard as you can, for unseen opportunities that will surely come. As much as I tried to anticipate the future, all along the way, my greatest career opportunities were ones that I never saw coming.

But public leadership is not easy . . .

I've seen authorized staffing levels in an upcoming fiscal year limited by the actual fill levels at some arbitrary point the year before. The justification? "That must be all the staff you need." Finally, I have experienced "fee-for-service" systems where the organization "made money" but was not allowed to reinvest any of the excess revenue to improve capability or performance. Retained earnings were routinely skimmed off to make up for deficits elsewhere.

To complicate the job of the public leader further, this driving of the agenda by elected officials sometimes results in frequent changes of direction, unreasonable requests such as deadlines in sync with election cycles, and occasionally, unworkable or impractical ideas. This is often greeted with resistance by the rank and file, who feel they have more than enough to do already, or that the people in charge don't know what they're doing.

If this isn't daunting enough, public leaders are watched closely. Public access to records has become universal. Most jurisdictions have laws that allow members of the public, and the media, to scrutinize and criticize everything and anything about a public organization. Dealing with these requests represents a significant burden.

Then, there are the so-called "control agencies." These are discrete entities in government whose role it is to provide general oversight; review performance; ensure compliance with policies, budgets, and executive orders; and guarantee adherence with statutes. In New York, we had the Division of Budget, the Office of the State Comptroller, the Department of Civil Service, and the attorney general at a minimum. Most large governments have similar offices, all designed to protect the taxpayer's interests.

On the federal level there are the Office of Management and Budget, the Office of Personnel Management, and the Government Accountability Office, just to name a few. These are entities the public leader has to deal with that his or her private-sector counterpart does not.

Probably the biggest problem facing the public leader falls in the category of personnel policy. While private firms have the ability to set job duties, salary and benefits, promotion guidelines, and employee evaluation and discipline systems, the public leader, in most cases, is hamstrung with a rigid, often archaic, set of rules. Fixed salary schedules, outdated classification systems, ineffective merit and seniority rules, and the lack of any real connection between pay and performance all make it extremely difficult to move a public organization forward.

The private firm can go after the best and brightest in a particular field, and compensate accordingly, but the public leader can pay only what the salary schedule allows. The business executive can rid the organization of nonperformers rather efficiently, while the public leader is usually burdened with a time-consuming and ineffective disciplinary process. Generally speaking, the public employee can get by with a minimal level of effort, while the rule in private business is "make your numbers" or go home.

It should be clear by now that it's not possible to simply run government like a business, and one should not expect to. However, that doesn't mean that public entities can't become efficient and effective, high-performing organizations that have all the look and feel of a successful private enterprise. It is possible. I've seen it.

The answer lies hidden in that bulk of talented people trapped in the middle of our public organizations who would welcome becoming part of something meaningful. But without leadership, these people have no choice but to labor day to day, stifled by the requirements and paralysis of an archaic one-size-fits-all bureaucracy. Absent real leadership, these folks must be satisfied with putting in their time, collecting their pay and benefits, and slowly rising through the ranks. Having no ownership in the cause, organizational performance is someone else's problem.

You will recall that this was the environment that welcomed me to the public sector, and it was just not my idea of a meaningful career. Sure, the job paid the mortgage and put food on the table, but it did nothing for my sense of self-worth. I wanted to do more. I needed to feel as if what I was doing mattered in some way.

This is what I believe is true not only for me, but for you, for all of us. It's simply about spending oneself in a purposeful, worthwhile endeavor—about being a contributing member of something that matters, something that one can be passionate about. I believe that this need for meaning in one's life, this basic individual desire for passionate contribution to a worthy cause, represents the holy grail for the transformational leader.

If you as a leader can capture the collective imagination of the organization, create a shared vision of a future state in which people can see themselves reaching their potential, finding their inner worth; if as a leader you can inspire a culture in which all people matter, in which all people can see themselves growing, contributing, and achieving something worthwhile, you will have unlocked the secret to true transformation. If you can touch that inner self that longs for passion, for meaning, and for purpose, you will unleash a power never thought possible in the public sector. If as their leader you touch their minds, hearts, and souls in this way, transformation will be at your fingertips.

But what does it take? Who is this leader who can rise above that maze I described earlier to liberate that mass in the middle and transform our public organizations from "one form of being into another"? My experience is that this special brand of leader is the one who demonstrates honest and sincere respect for all people, who frames and communicates inspiring vision, who stays the course with unwavering courage, who exhibits powerful intuition, and who is defined by unquestioned credibility and integrity. This is what the transformational public leader looks like. My goal is to help mold you in this likeness and image.

Let's talk first about respect, the prerequisite to all the rest.

Part II

Respect

CHAPTER 8

THE DINNER TABLE

Remember the little house in chapter 3, the one my parents built before "the war"? It was small, but as far as I knew at the time, it was a mansion, truly a great place to grow up.

As you might expect, all of the rooms were tiny, some more so than others. The "parlor" and dining room were okay, but our one bathroom was so small your back was pretty much against the wall as you stood at the sink. Most of our clothes were kept in a single closet less than two feet wide that my parents referred to as the "clothes press." And "press" them it did!

I did have my own bedroom, but it was so small that the twin bed touched three of the four walls and the door had to swing out into the hall. I had a small chest for socks and underwear and a little desk for homework.

One of the nicer features of our little place was the "sun parlor" on the south end of the house. With windows on three sides, it was a very pleasant space. The distinguishing feature of this room was the vast collection of porcelain, china, wood, plaster, glass,

Out of the Clay

and plastic dogs that my mother had acquired over the years and proudly presented on top of the long hot-water radiator. Unfortunately, when my sister, Carol, and I would take to horseplay, flying pillows and such ... Well, you get the picture.

But the room where most family time took place was the tiny kitchen. It had a counter along one wall with a sink in the middle under the window and "party-line" telephone hanging on the wall at the end. A freestanding gas stove and refrigerator were against an adjoining wall.

Taking up what scarce space was left was a metal-top table with wooden legs and wooden chairs, typical of the day. At dinner time, after the two "leaves" were extended from the long sides of the table, the room was very crowded. My father sat comfortably at the head of the table, but my mother had her back against the sink. I was backed up to the stove while my sister was squeezed between the table and the outside wall where she could, without detection, drop her brussels sprouts down into the back of her shirt by pretending to scratch her neck. After dinner, she would go into the bathroom to make them disappear for good. Just one of her many tricks.

Unbeknownst to my father, or to me at the time, it was at this cozy table in this tiny kitchen that he gave me my earliest lessons in leadership. As it would turn out, these were lessons that I drew upon throughout my career.

As was typical in middle-class America at that time, we all sat down around the dinner table every evening as a family. We had no television, smartphones, or other technological distractions, nor did we have to hurry off to any organized sports or activities. We would share with each other stories about our day at work, at school, or at play. I admired my father and listened intently to his stories.

In those early days, as I mentioned earlier, my father was a maintenance man at the county welfare home. He was responsible for keeping the heating, electrical, and plumbing systems of the physical plant in good working order. It was a hard, dirty, and sometimes dangerous job with very little pay. His eight-hour work schedule would rotate from days to afternoons to the midnight shift.

But the worst part of the job was the boss. He was very demanding, highly critical, and showed no respect or appreciation for my father or the work he did. As a consequence, my father was very unhappy and longed for the day when he could walk into Barringer's office, throw the keys on his desk, and quit on the spot.

I can remember, as if it were yesterday, the family dinner when my father proudly announced that he had done just that. You see, my father was an excellent mechanic with hands like iron who had skills in almost all the trades. But he had a special affinity for electrical work. He had made a commitment to himself that he would become a master electrician, and this would be his ticket out of the welfare home. After several years of study of the National Electrical Code, he passed his licensing exam on the first try, got a good job in a local paper mill, and was able to toss Barringer the keys.

It wasn't long before he leveraged the paper-company job into a position in our local Watervliet Arsenal. It was here that big "gun tubes" were produced for tanks and artillery pieces using a wide range of large, complex machinery, all of which needed the electricians to help set up and keep running. My father loved this job, and it provided much material for those dinner-table discussions. Having served in World War II, he was a patriot at heart and felt he was still serving his country by helping make the big guns.

The best stories centered around the occasional new piece of equipment that was brought to the shop that the engineers couldn't manage to get running correctly. The story usually ended with my father studying the complex schematics, diagnosing the problem, and bringing the new machine on line. To be honest, I wondered if these stories had been exaggerated until my sister, going through some old family papers recently, came upon a formal commendation my father had received. Apparently, he designed a modification to an experimental high-speed rifling machine to solve a problem that had baffled the engineers.

Following his retirement from the "gun shop," my father became a maintenance electrician at my alma mater. Again, we heard about the projects accomplished, the problems solved, the professors, department heads, his coworkers, and even the college president. His fifteen minutes of fame there usually centered around restoring electrical power to the five-thousand-seat RPI Field House after it had been lost in the middle of a standing-room-only ice hockey game.

On very rare occasions, these dinner-table stories would center on "the war," never the horror of it, usually just some entertaining anecdote. I remember one about him leading a convoy transporting urgently needed tanks to the front lines. They came upon an old bridge that the French wouldn't let them cross because all the charges were set for demolition. After lengthy negotiation and a promise to move cautiously, the "high sign" was given to the lead transport, which proceeded to come roaring down the hill and over the bridge followed by the rest of the convoy. I can still picture my father sitting at that table laughing almost uncontrollably as he described the French engineers running for their lives into the woods.

It wasn't until many, many years later that I realized that I had been receiving some important leadership training from someone who had not even graduated from high school. I have never forgotten those stories, and reflecting on them, I realized there was a single ingredient that linked all of the good bosses, the good managers, the good professors, and the good military officers: respect.

Why was my father hell-bent on throwing the keys on Barringer's desk and walking out? No respect! On the other hand, why was he willing to go above and beyond the requirements of his job to get that big machine running in the gun shop? Respect!

Yes, the common ingredient that defined these leaders was the respect they gave my father and everyone else in the organization who, in turn, worked hard for those who gave them that respect. And the higher the office of the person dispensing this respect, the more powerful it was.

The dinner-table stories made it clear that the recipients of such respect would follow their leaders anywhere and do whatever it took to get the job done. They just didn't want to let them down and consistently strove to exceed expectations.

It was primarily from this respectful treatment and appreciation of their work that their self-worth was fueled. I've already expressed my belief that self-worth is the holy grail of the transformational leader, and you can begin to see this at work in these stories and others that will follow. If you can capture or trigger that feeling within your followers, you can unleash untold human potential, and upon this foundation, you can build a true transformation.

I have never forgotten those stories that we shared around that dinner table so long ago. The leadership lessons they conveyed I carry with me to this day. Through these early lessons, I learned that respect is central, actually prerequisite, to any effort at transformation. If you don't lead with respect, they won't follow!

Chapter 9

Mamma Cried

He was going to be a general and build on a proud family tradition!

In the last chapter, I alluded to my father's service in World War II. Attached to General George Patton's Third Army, he was part of the push to Bastogne during the famous Battle of the Bulge. He came home with stomach ulcers, hemorrhoids, hearing loss, and a piece of shrapnel just below his right eye, but he always considered himself one of the lucky ones.

My wife's father, Bill Baker, also served in the European Theater in World War II. Another tough Irishman from south Troy, he was an MP with the 100th Infantry Division, well regarded for their victory in the Battle of Bitche.

In the Pacific, my wife's uncle, Jack Baker, was a supply sergeant assigned to the island of Tinian in support of the *Enola Gay*, the B-29 Superfortress bomber that dropped the atomic bomb on Hiroshima. A generation later, Jack Baker's son, Paul, would be killed in Vietnam while serving with the Unites States Marine Corps.

Out of the Clay

Finally, there was the service of Lieutenant Colonel William J. O'Brien and Sergeant Thomas A. Baker, two members of my wife's family who were posthumously awarded the Congressional Medal of Honor for heroism during the battle for the tiny Pacific island of Saipan. As members of Troy's own 105th Regiment, 27th Infantry Division, both were killed while holding off a banzai attack by the Japanese, allowing many of their men to escape.

Although my own service in Vietnam pales in comparison to the sacrifice of those who came before me, it did continue the family tradition. So you can certainly understand why we were filled with pride when our firstborn son received an appointment to the United States Military Academy at West Point. He was going to be a general. I was sure of it!

Our son had good grades, test scores, and extracurricular activities, but when he first expressed interest in the Military Academy, we still thought it to be quite a pie-in-the-sky goal. But after a long, rigorous process, the Academy offered him admission under the early-decision program and offers of appointment came from both our member of Congress and United States senator.

Taking your firstborn off to college is a big day under any circumstances. But when he actually reported to West Point on that hot first day of July, it was an intensely proud moment for our entire family. All in that first day, he was given a tight haircut, issued a set of uniforms, taught to march and salute, and appeared in formation in a parade on "The Plain." I was bursting with pride, but reflecting the emotion of the day, his mamma cried all the way home!

Among the things issued to him that first day was a tiny book called "Bugle Notes." This compact compendium contained a good deal of information that the new cadet had to memorize and be ready to recite on command of a first classman (firstie). Much of it was useless trivia such as the number of lights in Cullum Hall, the number of gallons in Lusk Reservoir, and the number of names on the Battle Monument on the Academy grounds.

But a good deal of it was useful information, such as the words to the alma mater, the army song, general orders, and the code of conduct. What impressed me the most, however, was the wealth of insights and inspirational quotes on leadership from noted military leaders of the past.

My favorite, and the one I found most useful in my own work, is a quote from Major General John M. Schofield, then superintendent of the Academy, in an address to the corps of cadets in 1879. This well-known quote is widely known as Schofield's Definition of Discipline:

> *The discipline which makes the soldiers of a free country reliable in battle is not to be gained by harsh or tyrannical treatment. On the contrary, such treatment is far more likely to destroy than to make an army. It is possible to impart instruction and to give commands in such a manner and such a tone of voice to inspire in the soldier no feeling but an intense desire to obey, while the opposite manner and tone of voice cannot fail to excite strong resentment and a desire to disobey. The one mode or the other of dealing with subordinates springs from a corresponding spirit in the breast of the commander. He who feels the respect which is due to others cannot fail to inspire in them regard for himself, while he who feels, and hence manifests, disrespect toward others, especially his inferiors, cannot fail to inspire hatred against himself.*

I cannot overemphasize how much my experience and observations align with these words of General Schofield. I have observed and worked for both kinds of leaders and have seen the results.

Some of these leaders were, indeed, tyrannical, ambitious, self-absorbed, power-hungry, praise-seeking individuals who somehow landed in positions of authority. It is hard to believe that I actually witnessed screaming, threatening, manipulative, and borderline abusive behaviors on the part of such people. I think some of them believed that leading by fear was the best way to go.

In those instances, my colleagues and I felt the fear and sensed the clear absence of respect. Such treatment causes a paralysis of sorts and actually prevents people from doing more than the minimum. One becomes afraid to act when risks are not rewarded and mistakes are punished. Such self-important leaders are usually ready to take credit for any success, but when things go wrong, there is always a hunt for the guilty, someone upon which to place blame.

I really don't like to admit this, but those of us who were mistreated privately hoped for things to go wrong for the tyrannical leader. We just hunkered down, tried to avoid trouble, and waited. Obviously, significant human potential and creative talent went untapped. Transformation would never be possible under such circumstances.

The alternative leaders were respectful, compassionate, and understanding! They never forgot where they came from and never exhibited any behaviors that suggested they were superior. They found ways to demonstrate respect for everyone so that we could not help but respect them in return.

Out of that respect, people strove to do their best work and make a contribution. People were willing to take risks to move the organization forward because success was recognized and celebrated, while any failure simply served as a learning or coaching opportunity. Such leaders were observed everywhere in the organization interacting, supporting, encouraging, and demonstrating real concern for what people were doing, not just as employees, but as human beings.

As I said in the preface, I've done some things right and done some things wrong, but learned from both. Early in my career, before I fully understood public employees and human behavior, I admit that I tried the tyrannical approach with certain individuals from time to time. It never worked! Not once! All it did was to make these people angry with me, and it did nothing to improve performance. They just hunkered down, moved just fast enough to avoid an insubordination charge, and waited until I disappeared.

Further, it made friends and colleagues of these people unhappy with me as well. My apparent show of disrespect created a desire on their part for me to fail, just as General Schofield warns. Things never got better while I used that approach.

As I mentioned in chapter 7, it is an unfortunate reality that the average public employee doesn't have to move much farther, work more effectively, or go any faster than they want to. But to achieve a transformation, you will need to lead them places they may not want to go, ask them to do things they may not want to do, and expect them to do it faster than they may want to move.

But the entrenched bureaucracy will not, and cannot, be transformed or reinvented through harsh or tyrannical leadership! The only hope you have is to have earned their undying respect, a respect and loyalty so strong that they will follow you anywhere. As Schofield's Definition suggests, the only sure route to such a level of respect is for them to fully understand, and believe in their hearts, that they have your undying respect as well.

In the next three chapters, I will introduce you to three of the most influential mentors I have had in my career, three transformational leaders who were defined by their respect for people. While each filled a uniquely different role, you will see the similarities in how the respect they demonstrated for people played out in their work and contributed to their success.

Read carefully and reflect often . . .

Chapter 10

Essere Humano

It was 2:00 a.m. and I was still wide awake staring at the ceiling. Even though I knew things would probably look better in the morning, I had no idea about what to do first.

This nightmare began with what appeared to be a very exciting opportunity, an appointment to the Board of Trustees at Hudson Valley Community College in Troy, New York. With strong science and technology programs, Hudson Valley was of particular interest to me, and since I had been a part-time instructor there while I was in graduate school, it was a special honor to return to the college as a trustee.

My appointment to the board grew out of a power struggle of sorts in the county legislature. This Republican-controlled body declared a number of vacancies on the board based on the technicality that several of the duly appointed trustees (Democrats) had not signed their oath of office within the statutorily required thirty days.

But the timing of this move couldn't have been worse, as the

Out of the Clay

college was in the midst of its five-year reaccreditation review by the Middle States Association of Colleges and Universities. Because of what Middle States deemed to be the "appearance of political interference" in the operation of the college, reaccreditation was deferred. This put the viability of the institution at great risk. Just as this happened, the chairman of the board resigned and I was elected to replace him—and the sleepless nights began.

These are the circumstances under which I met Dr. Joseph J. Bulmer, president of the college at the time. Dr. Bulmer was another tough "south Troy boy" who rose from humble beginnings to the top of his class at La Salle Institute and Rensselaer Polytechnic Institute, attaining a PhD in nuclear engineering. At one point in his career, as a scientist at the Knolls Atomic Power Laboratory in Niskayuna, New York, he was involved in a government contract for the development of nuclear propulsion under the watchful eye of "the father of the nuclear navy," Admiral Hyman Rickover. Having been appointed president of the college in 1979, he now found himself in one of the most challenging periods of his presidency.

He and I immediately bonded and began to face this crisis together. I had instant admiration and respect for the man and considered it an honor to have the opportunity to work with such an accomplished scientist and distinguished leader. I sensed his admiration and respect for me in return, and he quickly became one of the more important mentors I've had in my career. In public, I called him "Mr. President" and he called me "Mr. Chairman." But in private, I called him "Joe" and to him, I was "Billy."

Now, what we did and how we did it could be the subject of another book. Suffice it to say that our efforts were successful and accreditation was restored.

In this chapter, however, I want to focus on Joe Bulmer as a transformational public leader. I learned a great deal from him, and his influence significantly shaped the kind of leader I was to become. I will mention him from time to time in other stories, but for now, I just want to tell you about a little plaque he had hanging in his office that bore the Latin phrase *Essere Humano*, which means "to be human."

Dr. Lucille A. Marion, a good friend and former colleague at the college, explained to me that "Doc" (as some of his closest staff privately referred to him) described this phrase as meaning "in all things there must be humanity." He would point to the plaque and remind everyone that "we must never focus solely on the business at hand: we must remember and focus on the human side of the enterprise as well."

And this came to explain what I learned to be the very human side of Joe Bulmer. When I first met him, we became instant friends. He showed a sincere interest in me, my career, my family, my interests, and my aspirations. Initially, I thought that this was because I was the new chairman of the board, his "boss," so to speak. But it didn't take long to learn otherwise.

As I would spend time with him on the campus, either on informal visits or at official events, I saw that he had built this kind of relationship with everyone. Full professors, new instructors, grounds crew, custodial or kitchen staff, it didn't matter. He knew everyone's name, their spouse's name, and their kids. He knew if they were having health or other issues, and he knew if they were having new babies, graduations, or other life events worth celebrating. He attended wakes and funerals and visited people in the hospital, wishing them quick recovery and speedy return. I couldn't believe it when he walked into my own father's wake!

For key management staff, he was largely viewed as an invaluable mentor giving them strong principles to guide their work. At the same time, in spite of his high office and public visibility, he could be spotted occasionally picking up litter on the front lawn of the campus, setting the example for the total commitment to excellence he expected from all. It may have been the Rickover influence, but no task, no detail escaped his view or was so unimportant that it shouldn't be done well. He set high expectations, but held himself to the highest standards.

All of this was sincere! He clearly demonstrated his belief that

Out of the Clay

everyone deserved to be treated with dignity and respect. The custodian mopping the floor received no less respect than the chairman of the board. As I watched, I could sense the incredible respect people had for the man, and I could see that it grew out of the sincere respect they were sure he had for them. I think they would have followed him anywhere. Joe Bulmer certainly impressed upon me the critical role respect plays in leadership, and it forever shaped my approach to my own work.

But it has to be sincere! It has to be real! I was sharing these impressions of Joe Bulmer with a friend the other day who related a story to me that I found hard to believe. He told me about a high-level public executive with whom he was having an introductory lunch meeting. Partway into the lunch, the executive carefully slid a crumpled piece of paper out of his pocket and, holding it below the table, proceeded to ask my friend, "How are Alice and Mildred?" (the names of my friend's daughters). That's not sincere! What a knucklehead! Who wants to follow someone like that?

I've mentioned more than once, part of the message of this book is to encourage you to look around and always be alert for lessons that you can take back to your leadership role. An example from my own recent experience, which is appropriate here, occurred on a recent visit I made to the Winship Cancer Institute in Atlanta. I was headed up a wide stairway on my way to the coffee shop to get a cup of my favorite mocha latte with whipped cream when I noticed a quotation in large letters prominently displayed on the wall.

> *One of the essential qualities of the clinician is interest in humanity, for the secret of the care of the patient is in caring for the patient.*
> —Francis W. Peabody

Through a quick internet search, I learned that Dr. Francis Peabody was a well-known physician and teacher who was noted for his unusual relationship with his patients, one of true caring and concern. This quotation was taken from his often-referenced essay "The Care of the Patient," a writing that has become a standard part of medical education. Although emanating from the field of medicine, this quote rang just as true as it pertains to public leadership. Essentially, it is yet another way of saying "Essere Humano."

Our private-sector brethren have a bucket of tools of all kinds, "carrots and sticks," to drive performance in their organizations without regard for the human dimension. The public leader, on the other hand, must care, truly care, about the people in his or her charge. It has to be real! It has to be sincere! And it has to be based on the fundamental belief that everyone deserves to be treated with respect and dignity. Without this core belief, you cannot lead a transformation in the public sector. Don't waste your time trying!

In the next two chapters, I'll share the stories of a couple of other people who demonstrated this same core belief and how it played out in their leadership approach. In later chapters, I'll share some examples of how this understanding ended up showing itself in my own work.

Please read carefully and reflect often . . .

CHAPTER 11

A Picture's Worth a Thousand Words

Could you ever think it possible that a public-sector career that began with shoveling coal in the boiler plant of a state prison could eventually lead to the opportunity to head four major public agencies? Well, this is exactly what one of my most influential colleagues and mentors accomplished over his fifty years of public service.

I first met John C. Egan early in my career when he was at the bureau chief level. He had come to Albany, New York, in 1960 from his position at Dannemora State Penitentiary in the "north country" where he did, indeed, shovel coal onto a conveyor in the boiler plant. He became a member of the newly formed Office of General Services (OGS) in New York and was involved in the construction of the forward-looking State Office Building Campus.

Right from the beginning, Egan demonstrated outstanding

ability, and with minimal formal technical training, he rose through the ranks quickly, in fact, all the way to commissioner of general services, a four-thousand-plus-member organization at the time. Yes, he was an excellent manager and got things done. But I believe that it was his possession of the five key attributes I am writing about that led to his singular record of leadership.

Remember "the power of the dirty socks"? If anybody had such power it was John Egan, as he is the first public leader who taught me, and others, about human respect and dignity. He never forgot his humble beginning. Never forgot where he came from. Never forgot the people who helped him along the way or the people who were not as fortunate.

As in the case of Joe Bulmer, he was everywhere in the agency. He worked to know everyone personally and worked to learn about their families, their hobbies, and their aspirations. More than once, he popped into my office unannounced and asked in his soft, disarming voice, "How's it going, Will?" We'd have a chat for a few minutes, sometimes about family, sometimes about work, sometimes about the weather, and he'd be on his way. And you just knew it was real!

By the time he was appointed commissioner, I was a bureau chief myself and had the opportunity to attend his periodic "expanded staff meeting," where he and others provided updates on agency activity, performance, or policy.

One of the key elements of this meeting was the "end-of-the-system" reports. Prior to each meeting, Egan would assign several of us in bureau chief or higher positions to spend a day doing or shadowing the job of somebody in our units who was at the lowest level, the "end of the system," so to speak. We then needed to prepare a report and make a formal presentation at the next expanded meeting about what we saw and learned. This was evidence of Egan's respect and concern for what he called the "line workers," and it made clear his expectation that we would exhibit similar respect and concern. It certainly worked for me!

I often heard him make comments about managers who felt

they were above the rest by saying things like, "He hasn't ridden the bus lately!" He cared about people and he expected us to do the same. And there were little messages as well. The agency had conducted an annual golf outing, which typically was held in a location and priced such that it was a bit of an elitist event, attended primarily by higher-level managers and supervisors. When Egan became commissioner, the venue, pricing, and marketing were all changed to allow everybody to participate in this agency-wide event if they were so inclined.

He also went to great lengths to promote from within in order to build careers and reward good performance. He understood that one promotion near the top would have a ripple effect with numerous promotions down the line. He encouraged us to do this even if one of these promotions may be what he called "soft."

And finally, his efforts to attract, retain, and advance women and minorities was beyond anything that we had seen up to that point. He never forgot the people who helped him, and he wanted to create similar opportunities for others. He truly cared!

When he left OGS, he became executive director of the Dormitory Authority of the State of New York. He was later appointed as commissioner of the NYS Department of Transportation and eventually, chief executive officer of the Albany County International Airport Authority. Before he was all finished, he returned for a second stint as commissioner of general services, and eventually became president of the nonprofit Renaissance Corporation. If this weren't enough, he was dedicated to his community, serving on the boards of numerous local hospitals and civic organizations. An incredible public career, indeed!

But one of the simplest moves he made was one with the most powerful of messages. It happened when he was appointed commissioner of the Department of Transportation. This department in the early 1990s was one of the largest in New York State government with more than ten thousand employees who were responsible for five hundred thousand miles of roads and

Out of the Clay

twenty thousand bridges. It was an extraordinary workforce with the highest standards for design and maintenance of this enormous infrastructure.

Clearly, this large and complex department demanded the brand of leadership exhibited by John Egan. So it was an important honor to be named the commissioner of transportation, and it afforded special status in the government hierarchy. I can still remember what a big deal Commissioner J. Burch McMoran was at the time I began my public career. This was, indeed, a top public-sector job!

At the time of Egan's appointment, the department headquarters occupied a large building on the State Office Building Campus in Albany, the very complex that he helped build as a young man. The atrium lobby had an impressive display of portraits of all the previous commissioners who held this prestigious position over the years.

But Egan did not succumb to the ego boost that such success can bring. He didn't let it cloud his vision. Ignoring tradition and posterity, and foregoing the opportunity to add his portrait to this long line of distinguished public leaders, he had them all taken down.

Instead, he had the images of former commissioners replaced with photographs of rank-and-file department employees going about their daily work. Some were operating heavy equipment. Some were driving trucks. Others were plowing snow, surveying rights of way, cutting brush, striping the highway, or inspecting bridges.

I was fortunate enough to have a conversation with Egan about this just months before he passed away. He told me that he had a sign placed over the top of this collage that read, "Every DOT Employee Is an Important Person!"

That one statement summed up Egan's view of humanity. He never forgot where he came from, or how blessed he was to have the opportunities that came his way, or how the actual work gets done. No matter how high he rose, he never lost his humility or his respect for the line worker, the boots on the ground, so to speak. He never lost sight of these people as individual human beings with families, problems, aspirations, and dreams of their own.

Yes, a picture is worth a thousand words! Yet, in this case, it can all be summed up in just one: respect! This is probably the greatest lesson I took from John Egan as a mentor, and I believe it was the underlying key to his singular success as a transformational public leader. We all respected him and would follow him anywhere.

In the next chapter, I'll tell you about yet another influential mentor who exhibited this same brand of respect.

Read carefully and reflect often . . .

CHAPTER 12

SEARCH? WHAT SEARCH?

The "executive search" is usually a time-consuming, and often expensive, process. Unfortunately, it does not always yield the best candidate, or even one who can perform well in the position. I have actually seen cases where the search itself lasted longer than the selectee did in the job.

Nowhere is the search process more sacrosanct than in academia. Of course, for the selection of a college president or provost, one would hope for the process to be objective, careful, and thorough. But I once saw an eight-member panel convened to execute a search for a relatively low-level clerical position where the person selected left after a month.

Clearly, the search process is a valuable tool. But it needs to be employed with flexibility and judgment, and adapted to the unique requirements of any given situation. And sometimes, it isn't needed at all.

This was the case when I was president of the Board of Education in Averill Park, New York, and our superintendent of

Out of the Clay

schools told us that he was planning to retire. There would not be a search.

How was this possible? We need to back up quite a number of years to when John J. Thero was a twenty-eight-year-old social studies teacher. At that time, baby boomers were flooding the school, forcing the Board of Education to consider the establishment of a separate junior high school. One afternoon, the superintendent, Howard Fuller, came to Jack's classroom and asked him, in a very brief conversation, if he would be interested in being principal of this new entity, should it happen. Jack was surprised by this out-of-the-blue question, but said he would consider it.

Jack heard nothing for weeks until his phone rang at 11:00 p.m. one night. It was Superintendent Fuller letting him know that the school board had just authorized the new junior high school and appointed him principal. It is clear to me that Fuller recognized Jack as an extraordinary leader and was not going to take no for an answer. No search needed!

While the district suffered through three years of double sessions, Algonquin Middle School was being planned and built. This new building would house grades six through eight, and there was no question that Jack Thero would be its first principal. Right, no search needed!

I think it was in the early years of Algonquin Middle School that Jack Thero emerged as a transformational public leader. I was not involved at the time, but over the years, I learned how the staff that he brought together rallied around him and responded to his leadership.

They became highly motivated, were outstanding in their work, and loved what they did. If you will pardon this one, overworked cliché, they became family. And as a result, the school quickly developed a reputation for excellence, experienced great student achievement, and, quite frankly, garnered the pride of the entire Averill Park community. Jack Thero and his team put Algonquin Middle School on the map!

How is it that one person, one leader, can be responsible for such success? How is it that employees can come to love or admire a leader such as Jack Thero and be willing to follow him anywhere and do whatever he asks? How can a school administrator achieve rock-star status in a community? One word: respect!

I first heard the name Jack Thero when there was a significant movement in the community at that time urging the school board to appoint him superintendent. A long-term, beloved gentleman was retiring from the position, and many felt that Jack was the right person for the job. Ultimately, the board went with a more experienced candidate.

But after joining the school board myself, I had the opportunity to experience him firsthand and learned that what I had been told had not been exaggerated. He was the consummate public leader who had earned the respect of faculty, students, parents, and the community at large. For me, he became an instant role model, exhibiting the leadership characteristics I hoped that one day I could achieve.

It quickly became clear that the key to the respect that he received was the respect he gave, just as Schofield suggests. And he did this in many ways.

First of all, he let his teachers know that he was proud of them. Formal evaluations contained lots of positive reinforcement as well as good coaching suggestions. Teachers never felt like they had done anything wrong. It was always, "Great job, and here's how you might get even better!"

He frequently stopped by classrooms and made informal observations as well. Teachers often found little notes in their mailbox from Jack telling them how impressed he was with something they had done. One retired teacher with whom I spoke still cherishes a collection of these Post-it Notes that she received. She said that it was clear he knew who you were, what you were doing, and that he cared.

Jack Thero was always visible and accessible. He took the time to walk around the building every morning greeting teachers and students alike. He knew everyone by name and used it. "Good morning, Mrs. Nicolas." "Good morning, Dr. Thero." And so it went with Mrs. Anthony, Mrs. Bligh, and all the rest.

He knew the names of spouses and kids, and knew about significant events or activities going on in their lives. He celebrated with them at the good times and showed genuine concern when they were experiencing problems or difficulties. His concern was real and it was hard work.

It would have been easier to cloister himself in his office reading the morning news or checking yesterday's sports scores. But that wouldn't have conveyed the respect he had for his staff, and he likely wouldn't have received much respect in return.

He was always available for teachers when they had a problem or needed some guidance. He knew how to listen, how to really listen. One teacher told me that "a blue-eyed stare right in your eyes made you believe you were the only thing important to him at that moment."

He didn't come to these conversations with preconceived ideas and was open to suggestions and feedback. He had a collaborative approach rather than authoritarian. Teachers knew that their opinions mattered and that they were part of the decision process.

He could offer a counter opinion without being disagreeable, and he always kept emphasis on the positive. Staff knew that they really mattered, and it enhanced their feeling of self-worth. Consequently, they held him in high esteem and didn't want to let him down.

As did my other mentors, Jack Thero consistently modeled the behaviors he expected from everyone else. He dressed professionally, spoke professionally, and treated everyone in a professional manner. Yet he did not consider himself above anyone, just part of the team, or family. More than once, he was seen picking up a piece of paper that was dropped in the hall or attending to some other detail of the physical plant. Such action did not go unnoticed by students or staff.

The community got to know him mostly through the interactions parents had with him. During back-to-school nights and

Out of the Clay

The underlying theme that threaded its way through all of our conversations was simply "respect." And so it was with the full support of all the key stakeholders that we appointed one of the finest public leaders I have ever met.

During Jack Thero's entire tenure as superintendent, I continued to serve as president of the Board of Education. He and I experienced a truly wonderful professional and personal relationship. I learned a great deal from him and continually aspired to be the kind of inspirational leader he was.

Many years after he retired, I met him at a social function and was able to tell him that oftentimes, when I encountered difficult work situations, I asked myself, "What would Jack do?" Need I say more?

other events, Jack Thero was as present, as professional, and as positive as he was during the school day. He worked hard to learn the names of parents and as much of their story as he could to show them that he cared about them as well, that they mattered too.

He was probably at his best during the resolution of difficult discipline situations where he showed both student and parent respect by listening attentively, and patiently moving the conversation forward in as positive a way as possible, truly seeking to understand their point of view. He never locked himself in his office to avoid conflict, as he viewed these situations as learning opportunities for everyone involved, himself included. But he always had the teacher's back, and any opportunities for their improvement were discussed privately.

I could go on, but I think I've said enough for you to understand why we were heartbroken when he announced that he was leaving to become the superintendent of schools in a smaller school district a bit further south in the Hudson River Valley. This represented a great leadership opportunity for him, and so with mixed emotions, off he went, leaving impossible shoes to fill.

Now, fast-forward five years to when our superintendent at that time told us of his impending retirement. After we got over the shock and caught our collective breath, the seven members of our board had the same idea at the same time. Honestly, I can't remember who said it first, but the more we talked about the idea of simply hiring Jack Thero, the more obviously right that idea was. Search? What search? We didn't need one!

Our first call was to Jack himself to check his interest in "coming home" to Averill Park. He said yes without hesitation. And in his usual way, he was flattered and humbled by the invitation. We then, in turn, met with leadership of the administrators group, the faculty association, the noninstructional staff, and key community groups. There wasn't the slightest hesitation, reservation, or objection from any of them to appointing Jack Thero as our new superintendent.

Chapter 13

Get a Handle on It!

If you are observant, you can even take important leadership lessons from fictional characters, like Major General Edward "Ned" Bracken, for example.

As I recall, it was an old WWII movie that I saw many years ago. Bracken was just put in command of a hard-luck army division with a poor record in combat. On the front lines in Europe, his mission was to make this unit battle ready by improving discipline, performance, and morale; transform it, so to speak.

The hard-nosed general began by demanding discipline and conformance to policy and procedure. Of course, this was met with much grumbling among the troops, that is until his men began to see the general actually in the trenches, right alongside them. He modeled the discipline and courage he demanded of them, but also showed that he cared about them and what they were doing.

One of the most instructive scenes showed a long line of troops waiting their turn for a grumpy old mess sergeant to unceremoniously dole out some sort of unidentifiable slop into the metal mess kits of each soldier. One after the other, the kits were filled and the soldier was told to "move it!"

After a bit, we notice General Bracken standing in the chow line waiting his turn to be "served." When he reaches the big pail of slop, the caught-off-guard sergeant salutes and yells to subordinates in the rear, "Get some food up here for the general." But Bracken declines and insists on having the same "food" as his men. After one taste, he dumps his mess kit out, tips the entire pail over onto the ground, and to loud cheers from the troops, orders the mess sergeant, "Get some real food for these men!"

We don't have to be in a war, or even in the military, to employ the powerful lessons of this fictional story. I actually used General Bracken as inspiration when I was appointed the director of the Department of Environmental Services in Arlington County, Virginia.

One of the larger bureaus in the department included all of the line workers who were responsible for the county's water, sewer, and street systems. In general, these were hard, dirty, dangerous jobs, critical for the health, safety, and welfare of the county. In fact, prior to my tenure, this bureau experienced an on-the-job fatality at a major water-main break.

As a new department head, I wanted the men and women in this bureau to know that I respected them and appreciated the hard work that they did. So early on, I made an informal visit to their headquarters. I went unaccompanied by any staff, as I think that sends a message of sincerity and humility. Further, people are more willing to speak more openly in such a setting.

I took my time and wandered through the building, chatting with many people who were, quite frankly, surprised to see me there. I learned things about what they did and how they did it, and was able to discuss my vision for the department. As luck would have it, I was able to connect with Reggie, one of the key leaders among the line workers, and we engaged in a fruitful conversation.

As we both sensed a feeling of trust developing, Reggie asked if he could show me something. Of course, this is what I was hoping for, and I let him lead me downstairs to the locker room.

The first thing he showed me was a large gang sink intended for the crews to wash up, removing the heavy-duty grease and grime that is so much a part of their work. The problem was, it hadn't worked for a couple of years and the crews had to struggle using a single, small, residential-style sink over in a corner. Apparently, complaints and requests to repair the big handwashing sink had been somehow absorbed into the bureaucracy.

The second thing he showed me was the mud room adjacent to the locker room. The mud room had a large, steel grillwork on the floor, which was designed to help the crews scrape the heavy mud off of their boots when they returned from a dirty job in the streets. This was much like the grates at the entrance to a ski lodge, but designed for mud rather than snow.

I was very impressed with this until Reggie took me through a door that led outside. Much to my surprise, the door had no handle on the exterior. The crews could not enter directly into the mud room as designed and, instead, had to traipse across the usually spotless tile lobby floor in their muddy boots to get into the locker room. I was speechless! Reggie explained that he thought the hardware was removed from the exterior to prevent pilfering of ice from the ice maker located right inside the door. And again, complaints had just evaporated.

I thanked Reggie for his time and told him that I would look into these matters. I told him that he didn't need to worry about my using his name or throwing him in with his superiors. He was a number of levels down in the department, and I didn't want to send the chain of command into a tizzy, possibly thinking I was "searching for the guilty," because I was not.

However, I did view this as a very important opportunity to send a clear message that the department was under new leadership, leadership that cared about, and respected, the men and women who worked there. It was a perfect chance for me to show how I thought people should be treated.

Out of the Clay

As soon as I returned to the office, I met with my operations chief. I told him how much I appreciated the line workers and how I thought we should send a message of respect to them by making sure their facilities were up to par. Even though full renovation of the building was not possible at this point, I asked that things like light fixtures, ceiling tiles, carpet and floor tile, restrooms, counters, and other quality-of-life items were free of visual or functional problems.

As the chief was leaving, I asked him not to miss the gang-sink problem and, with respect to the mud-room door, "Please, get a handle on it!" He didn't ask how I knew about these things but completed the survey quickly. Some $250,000 worth of remediation was identified and addressed. We even invited the trades workers who used the sink to select the style and location of the new one.

Providing a safe and pleasant work environment and getting your people the tools and training they need to do their jobs is a sign of respect. It shows you care about them as people and it helps earn their respect in return.

Another trip to the "end of the system" was to the scene of a water-main break that had several streets blocked and traffic diverted. As I pulled my county vehicle with flashing lights around the barricade and into the blocked-off street, the first people to see me wondered who this could be. All the usual participants were already there. Indeed, they were shocked, and pleased, to see the department director step out of the SUV.

As I walked up into the thick of things—trucks and noisy equipment in every direction, more barricades, more flashing lights, mud, water running down the street, and a gaggle of workers in hard hats, boots, and reflective safety clothing—I could sense an unusual energy. I could sense immediately that these people knew what they were doing, liked what they were doing, and were proud of what they were doing. It was clear to me that they understood the direct connection between their work and the health and safety of the residents on the street.

As luck would have it, Reggie was on the scene, along with his bureau chief, and they were both more than happy to answer my many rapid-fire questions. I was genuinely interested in what they were doing and how they did it, and they knew it. They were especially happy to demonstrate the advanced technology they had that helped them identify the exact location of the break. I guess I knew this, but where the water comes out of the ground and where the water line is broken are not necessarily the same place.

After allowing them to explain everything that was going on out there, I asked them if there was anything they needed to do their jobs better or more effectively. They immediately described a piece of equipment that would help them more accurately isolate the area of the break and keep water on to more homes and businesses while the break was being repaired. They explained the technology of how it worked, and as I recall, the cost was relatively modest. I asked them to complete their research and I authorized procurement of it on the spot. I promised I would follow this through the process until they had this new equipment in their hands.

The big message here: I see what you do! I care what you do! And I respect you for doing it!

And then, there was my snowplow ride. That's right! One morning, following a rare heavy snowfall the day and night before, I showed up at the Trades Center, again unannounced and unaccompanied, and said I'd like to ride with one of the drivers as they plowed the streets of the county. So, for the next several hours, I got to see what it was like maneuvering this large snowplow through mostly residential streets as people were digging out from the storm. The driver was in disbelief that he was driving the department head around and was all too willing to teach me about the equipment, how it worked, tricky parts or problems involved, and how teams of plows coordinated their efforts in their assigned sector of the county.

Again, I see what you do, and I care!

On one of my visits to the equipment shop, I took a closer look at the various trucks that I had seen around the county. Some were rather new, white trucks with the updated, slick-looking Arlington County logo on the doors, part of the county's rebranding program. But other trucks looked like junk. They were a dirty beige color with rusted-out fenders, deteriorating bodies, and the old "public works" logo on the doors. My investigation revealed that there was significant money in the budget for the replacement of much of this old equipment, but a conservative approach toward expenditures had delayed the process.

Now, I am conservative myself when it comes to budgeting and spending the public's money. But once justifiable expenditures are budgeted for, I believe in spending the money for its intended purpose, especially when it is for the tools people need to do their jobs. It not only helps them do their jobs well, it communicates care and respect, which can fuel performance beyond expectations. And so it was that I directed the acceleration of the acquisition of as many new trucks and other equipment as we could find money for and asked that we step up our budgeting in the coming years to complete the inventory as soon as possible.

With respect to the older trucks that were still in good condition and would be around for a while, I looked into painting them white to match the new trucks, but it was not cost effective. However, I had the old "public works" logos removed from the doors of the old beige trucks in favor of the new, well-designed Arlington County logo in order that all of our staff were sporting the same "brand" and felt a valued part of one organization. This was not a big or complicated thing to do, but it communicated a big message, and important message. Respect!

I could go on with more Arlington examples or enumerate the extensive technology and equipment we made sure our architects, engineers, and technicians had back at the Office of General Services in New York, but I think I've made my point. Show your people that you see and understand what they do, that you care about what they do, and that you respect them enough to get them the tools they need to do the job well. This will help you earn their respect in return.

Chapter 14

All about the Buzz

I can still remember how hot and humid it was! Quite unusual for early July! But the weather couldn't dampen my enthusiasm, as it was time for my first trumpet lesson, a moment I had been dreaming about for a very long time.

Third grade was behind me now, and I was quite pleased that I would never again have to see my least-favorite teacher of all time, Miss Wright. My new trumpet had been delivered a few weeks prior, but all I had been able to do was hold it and pose in front of the mirror. Blowing air into it accomplished nothing but the sound of wind.

Bell Top, the two-room schoolhouse where I had earlier attended first and second grade, was about a mile from home up the very steep Reynolds Road hill. Waiting for me there was old Mr. Morse, one of the high school music teachers, who was giving beginning brass lessons.

I was only eight years old but I remember it well, especially the great revelation that the sound of a brass instrument is actually created by the buzzing lips of the musician. "It's all about the buzz," said Mr. Morse. The brass horn just improves the quality of the sound.

But the most indelible image of that day is that of my seventy-two-year-old grandmother walking me up that steep hill. The school was far beyond the creek at Jordan Road, the southern perimeter of where I was allowed to walk alone, so my grandmother was along for security. I can still see her in her long "house dress" with a little round hat sitting on top of her piled-up snow-white hair, her small wire-rimmed glasses, her handbag dragging alongside, and her black tie-up shoes with the chunky heels. At about four foot ten, she really was the picture of the iconic "little old granny" of the time. Were it not for "Nanny," my music career may have never gotten off the ground.

And so, it was quite appropriate that she was there that beautiful evening the following spring when, after another nine months of weekly lessons and hours of practice, I was ready for what would be my first trumpet solo before an audience. I was elated, and it was somehow critically important to me that she bear witness to this moment in my life and to my accomplishment.

Accompanied by piano, I played a short rendition of an old English love song, "In the Gloaming," which, quite by coincidence, had been one of my grandmother's favorite songs when she was a young woman. My parents told me that Nanny, with a tear in her eye, quietly sang the words to herself while I offered a flawless performance. Then, on the way home, she slipped me a couple of bucks for doing such a good job. Money, I'm sure, she could ill afford to take from her meager social security check.

The key point here is the need I had for her to witness what I had achieved. You have probably had the same experience where it was important to you to have someone bear witness to something in your life. Maybe it was a school play, a ball game, or a science project. Or maybe it was a big event such as a graduation or an event as small as a new bike. Nonetheless, the need was there.

As my wife and I raised our own three children, they had the same need. Of course, we went to all the obvious things, the plays, the concerts, the games, and the like. But at one point, our middle school son was taking a field trip to a museum near where I worked at the time. He asked if I could come by during his class trip "so you can see us!" What a simple request. How important for him, and how easy to fulfill.

We recently attended a tee-ball game in which our five-year-old grandson, Will, was participating. We were in the bleachers along the third-base side, screened from the batter by the fenced-in dugout, when he came up to bat. After surveying the crowd, he left the batter's box and walked down the third-base line to where we were sitting, essentially stopping the game. He then instructed us to move down and stand behind the backstop "so you can see me!" After we moved, he stepped back in and the game resumed. He hit the ball and was thrown out at first. But undeterred, he rounded first base and headed into center field, where he stood until a coach carried him back to the dugout. Hilarious!

My experience suggests that we, as fully grown adults, are no different than kids when it comes to the need to have someone else bear witness to our accomplishments, to our work, and to our lives. Regardless of our role in life, from executive to laborer, we all need to be "seen" and appreciated for who we are and what we contribute. It is critical that we be validated in this way.

It's important to recognize that people work at their jobs day in and day out with the same people on the right and left, the same people above and below. The vast majority of them are proud of what they do and their families are proud of them for doing it. But to fully engage them and have them inspired to reach higher, a prerequisite for transformation, they need to know that they are doing something more than just coming to work, plying their trade, and making a living.

What this presents for the leader is a golden opportunity to be the witness to the people in the organization and the work they

Out of the Clay

do. To have a division chief, a principal, a superintendent, a department head, a deputy commissioner, or other top official show up in the offices, the shop, the classroom, the street, a project site, or wherever work is going on goes a very long way to demonstrate respect and earn it in return, mutual respect that is critical in leading a transformation. I've learned from experience on both the giving and receiving end of the informal, unannounced, one-on-one visit that it is a very powerful leadership tool.

In earlier chapters I introduced you to John Egan, Joe Bulmer, and Jack Thero, all masters of the informal visit. All three demonstrated respect by bearing witness to the people in their organizations, and they earned respect in return.

With John, Doc, and Jack as role models, I made every effort to follow this practice. I have to admit that I wasn't always good at it. As is the case with most people in executive positions, paperwork, meetings, phone calls, and the like make it extremely difficult to escape from the office. Getting out to visit where the work was getting done was never urgent, but as time went on, I grew to understand just how very important it is.

The more I followed this practice, the better I got at it and the stronger were the relationships I was building, especially when I stopped for no reason whatsoever at a place that my predecessors generally did not go. I slowly started to understand that these visits created a "buzz" that compounded the benefit well beyond the one-on-one visits themselves.

For example, on one occasion in Arlington, I stopped into the cubicle of one of our transportation engineers, introduced myself, and started a chat. Pointing to a set of drawings on her desk, I began to ask questions about her project. She was more than happy to explain to me what she was doing and how she was doing it. I learned a great deal about traffic standards that day and she, on the other hand, felt more recognized and valued. Before the end of the day, I got wind that people were talking about this simple act of respect. There was a buzz!

On another occasion, I had a call from another department

head who asked me, "What did you do down at the Trades Center?" When I sounded confused, she said, "I've heard you are a hero out there! Something about turning the water on." Apparently, my efforts to get the crew the gang sink they needed had an impact far beyond the people who were using it. Again, there was a buzz!

I've already told you about my wandering through the Trades Center, visits to the equipment shops, stopping at water-main breaks, and riding on the snowplow, among others. And people talked about all of it. Every visit helped build the "buzz" about my respect and concern for the people in the organization regardless of rank or role.

Not unlike my need to have my grandmother attend my first concert, people want and need to be validated. The more that can be done by the leader, the more possible transformation becomes. Although I made every effort to get out of my office and see what people were doing, it never seemed enough. I often received the feedback, "We'd like to see Bill more!" You, too, will probably not be able to get out there as much as you or your people would like. But rest assured, word of the visits you do make will spread. In the words of my old music teacher, "It's all about the buzz!"

Chapter 15

Mountains out of Molehills

Spring was a wonderful time as kids. It meant baseball, bike riding, and spring blossoms.

It also meant the annual trip to Cooper's on Third Street in downtown Troy to get our new shoes for Easter. This unique store had a pit of sorts all around the perimeter where the salesman was able to stand in front of loaded shelves and try a shoe on your foot without bending over. Then there was the "x-ray" machine where you could stand and look through a viewer to see how your toes fit inside your shoes. Great fun! After all these years, I can still feel the pain of those new, stiff leather shoes and remember walking around the house with watering eyes trying to break them in.

Easter Sunday Mass was always beautiful. Everyone was dressed in their fine new clothes; women in fancy hats with fresh corsages, men with starched shirts, new ties, and crisp fedoras, and little girls in their brightly colored dresses. I usually had a new suit, shirt, and clip-on tie to go along with those new stiff leather shoes. Memorable!

The Easter celebration always included plenty of sugary treats. Usually a big chocolate rabbit in the middle of a large basket surrounded by chocolate eggs, marshmallow chickens, and dozens of jellybeans hidden in the green plastic "grass." The yellow chickens were, and still are, my favorite.

Then there was the obligatory photo op in front of the rose bushes after church. These photos were taken with our trusty Brownie box camera, and at a distance such that it was almost impossible to tell who was in the picture when it was developed.

In any case, these fuzzy photographs became of increasing value as time went on. They did mark key milestones in life and tracked how we grew, changed, and developed over the years. I guess it was a little sad when we outgrew the annual Easter photo shoot. But this was replaced by other opportunities to record life as it rolled on, such as concerts, plays, proms, and graduations. I think it is of great importance to us as human beings to record these milestones for posterity.

I believe there are similar milestones in our work lives that are important to record for posterity. My earliest experience comes from my time in the military, where being commissioned as an officer in the United States Army was a big deal for me and appropriately photographed for posterity. Later, promotions to first lieutenant and captain were similarly recorded. I know I felt important at each of those milestones, and the people around me, and those who arranged for these events, made me feel important and valued.

This sort of thing is a powerful way to recognize people and make them feel not only valued, but respected. In Arlington, I invited every person who was being promoted in my department to come to my office, accompanied by their chain of command. I would gather as much information as I could about the person beforehand in order that I could conduct a meaningful conversation and, indeed, make it personal.

I would talk about the person's family, hobbies, and favorite sports teams, their role in the organization, and how that fit our mission and vision. I would then make a formal presentation of the promotion letter and talk about what the person had done to deserve it. I made sure that photographs were taken and distributed to all in attendance.

Now, think back for a moment to the dinner table conversations I enjoyed when I was a kid. Then think about the stories you are creating for these people of today to carry home. Think about how this newly promoted person is able to describe the very special day they had at work. Without warning, they were summoned to the "big boss's" office and had nice things said about them. They were told how important they are to the organization, were handed a promotion letter complete with an increase in compensation, and all of it documented in a photograph for posterity.

To the high-level manager, this may seem like making mountains out of molehills, but to that individual, it's a big deal! To the person being recognized, this is one of those key "photo-in-front-of-the-rose-bush" moments that records life as it rolls along. Witnessing it in this way and celebrating it with the individual builds respect, loyalty, and trust, essential elements for a transformation. This person is now far more likely to follow you as a leader, even if it is somewhere they do not necessarily want to go.

The transformational leader can find ample opportunity to create such celebratory events and mark moments that are big for the individual and the individual's family. Obtaining a professional license, becoming certified in some area of technical endeavor, or even receiving a service award from a community or volunteer organization all present opportunities to celebrate. Over the years, I did my best to give people positive stories to take home to the dinner table and a photograph to put on the mantel or in an album. And as in the case of the promotion celebrations, I watched this practice further build respect, loyalty, and trust.

Growing up in a blue-collar family, I understood the importance of tools and how personal they can become. And so it was with this understanding that I pushed hard for the replacement of outdated trucks and equipment that I mentioned in chapter 13. I understood the pride the men and women who worked in the streets took in their work and in their equipment.

As we received the deliveries of new trucks, I arranged for a big celebration and photo op at one of our parks facilities. We lined up all the shiny new trucks military style, with the drivers and assistant drivers standing in front, and took a lengthy series of photographs. We took group shots, close-up shots of drivers with their trucks, and pictures of me inspecting trucks as the drivers explained them to me. I shook hands with everyone and congratulated them on receiving their new equipment.

Copies of photographs were provided to all participants and they all had a great story to take home. During this event, you could sense the increasing respect, loyalty, and mutual trust. You may think this is making mountains out molehills, but this is their work, their life, their day in and day out. To them, this is everything!

But it doesn't always have to be a big celebration. Sometimes a simple thank-you or pat on the back will do. One year, after receiving my annual evaluation from a boss I greatly respected, he asked me what he could do better. I said, "Say thank you once in a while." After the shock wore off, he asked me, "Why? People are getting paid to do their jobs!" I explained that if he was satisfied with people doing their jobs, then his approach was okay. But if he wanted people to rise up and exceed expectations, they needed to feel the respect conveyed in an extra thank-you or message of appreciation.

Like so many aspects of leadership, it's just not rocket science. A little note in a mailbox or stuck on a door, simple refreshments before a staff meeting, a letter home, a pen or other token recognizing a special contribution or extra effort, or a simple thank-you written on the corner of a piece of staff work returned all translate into one simple word: respect!

The stories you send home are critical and play a key role in unlocking the full potential of the organization. If a person's family senses the respect their loved one is receiving at work, they too are more likely to be supportive of the organization and the role their loved one is playing in it. The workers who have the encouragement and support of their families are going to be far more loyal and productive than those who don't.

On the other hand, I have observed disgruntled employees whose agitation was exacerbated by an angry spouse or other family member who felt there was lack of respect or fair treatment at work. This family support is especially critical during the difficult periods of transformation when people are asked to go above and beyond, to go where they have not gone before and do what they have not yet done.

So while the ordinary manager pays no attention to such things, the transformational leader, who truly respects the staff, will dip into the stream of events and take advantage of every opportunity to, yes, make mountains out of molehills. It says: I know what you do! I recognize your accomplishments and contributions! I care about you and I respect you. This is another opportunity where the leader can tap into that holy grail of self-worth and unleash its potential to build the respect it takes to have people follow you anywhere.

Chapter 16

The Damn Dog!

When my wife-to-be and I were first dating, her family had a little dog, a purebred wirehair terrier, "The Duke of Meadowbrook." Duke had been a gift to my wife's little brother from her godfather, who believed that "every boy should have a dog."

Wanting to be favored by the family, I tried hard to befriend Duke, who barked and growled at me whenever I came in the house or got anywhere near him. Although he looked cute, he really was an obnoxious little thing, and all efforts to build a peaceful relationship with him failed. I guess he never liked me, and truth be told, I didn't care so much for him either.

And so, it was a happy day when I learned that my future mother-in-law, Lu Baker, wasn't fond of the little guy either. Whenever she spoke of Duke, her statements always referenced "the damn dog." She had not suggested a dog and was not at all happy when he arrived. With four kids to raise and a home to take care of, she didn't need all the extra work that a dog entails.

Out of the Clay

Simply put, Lu Baker found Duke to be nothing but a major annoyance.

I need to point out here that Lu Baker, a gracious descendent of the Whalen clan, had a significant repertoire of sayings. Some were, indeed, Irish sayings that had been passed down through the generations, while others were of her own creation. For example, when the kids were bugging her about "What's for dinner?", they were sometimes told "codfish and snowballs" or "nyet nyet on toast." She had a seemingly endless list of these original, humorous retorts, and she would be proud that many of them are alive and well in our family today.

But one of my favorites related to Duke. As she went about her daily and weekly activities, both inside and outside the home, Lu Baker had to interact with many people, including friends, neighbors, store clerks, work associates, and the like, along with the occasional family member, sometimes even "Crazy Aunt Ruth." (Hey, everybody's got one!)

As you might expect, she would encounter the occasional gossip, lack of cooperation, dishonesty, undependability, unwanted advice, and many of the other kinds of common, but annoying, human behavior or interference we all experience. And when she did, Lu Baker had at the ready, "The more I see of people, the better I like Duke!"

As the passionate, dedicated, totally committed transformational leader, you are going to have days where everybody drives you crazy and you wish you had known Duke yourself. I know I still, from time to time, find it necessary to reach back for this useful phrase of Lu Baker's.

It is just a fact of the human condition that even the best staff will, from time to time, be annoying. It is normal for them to make the occasional mistake, lose focus, forget something important, exhibit poor judgment, and so on. Figuratively speaking, in their interactions with you, with customers, or with each other, they will sometimes bark, growl, need to be groomed or fed, or make messes that will have to be cleaned up. And you can't just scold them or throw them away every time something like this happens. Lu Baker never kicked the dog down the stairs, and neither can you.

The challenge for you is to deal with these annoyances without losing respect for your people or doing it in a way that they lose respect for you. After all, they, you, and I are just human, and the success of your transformation efforts will depend greatly upon your ability to embrace this humanity and maintain honor, dignity, and respect for all.

I know how it feels when someone brings to your attention something that has gone horribly wrong. I remember a project where our contractor got his equipment too close to an historic structure and it collapsed. Or the time we executed a contract for the demolition of a building on which we had just completed an exterior paint job. Or consider the large water-main pipe for a sprinkler system that was run right through the middle of the plush office of the institution director. And finally, the clerical error that resulted in a contractor being overpaid by several million dollars. In each case, I just wanted to throw my hands up! Who was watching the store?

But rather than hunt for the guilty, affix blame, and inflict punishment, such "malfunctions" must be viewed as learning opportunities. Your people are human, and even the best will mess something up once in a while. You need to work with them in a respectful manner as you talk about how things could have been done differently or better. An employee who has made a mistake but is treated with respect by the boss is far more likely to pay that back by trying much harder the next time.

In chapter 12, I told you about Jack Thero and the relationship he had with his teachers. Do you think for a minute that they did everything right all the time? Of course not. But no matter what had happened, he would tell the teacher what had worked well and then respectfully discussed how it could be even better the next time. They never felt they were criticized or put down.

My father-in-law, Bill Baker, an outstanding public executive in his own right, uniformly preached "emphasis on the positive." No matter what had transpired, he searched first for the good and put the emphasis on that. There was always time later to identify and discuss opportunities for improvement.

Remember the plaque in Doc Bulmer's office, "Essere Humano!" — in all things there must be humanity. My observation and experience suggest that this is, maybe, the most critical of all the attributes of the transformational leader.

So, now they're ready to follow — but where are they to go?

Part III

Vision

Chapter 17

The Jungle

I've spent the first sixteen chapters of this book talking about my story and about the role of respect in transformational leadership. But I have not talked about management, nor done more than hint that there is a difference between the manager and the leader. It's time to address that difference.

Over the years, I have read many explanations of this difference, but for me, there is one metaphor that says it most clearly. I think I first read a version of this in the writings of Stephen Covey.

The setting is in a jungle where a crew has the mission of cutting a path. First there are workers who actually produce something: cutting the brush, loading the debris, maintaining the wagons, and so on. Then there are the managers who monitor and analyze production and performance; arrange for equipment, food, and other supplies; set up work schedules; and organize training.

But where is the leader while all this is going on? The leader is up in the top of a tree pointing, "This way!"

Out of the Clay

I think this one factor is the most important in distinguishing between a manager and a leader—VISION! It's the leader's role to see the big picture, to see far down the road, to anticipate the future and the inherent ramifications to the organization.

The leader must understand the core purpose of the organization and continually evaluate its relevancy in light of the current and anticipated environment within which the organization functions, especially the threats and opportunities. The leader needs to see the strengths of the organization as well as its vulnerabilities. I've heard it said that managers see that things are done right; leaders see that the right things are done. I agree!

I know this may sound like the typical SWOT analysis (strengths, weaknesses, opportunities, and threats) that happens routinely in a consultant- or facilitator-led off-site retreat. I'm sure you've seen them, attended by a group of select individuals who are tasked with developing a strategic plan for the organization. But it's not! You see, such a group looks like, sounds like, and in my opinion, very often gets results similar to a committee.

Early in my career, a very seasoned executive taught me the definition of a camel: "a horse designed by committee!" Later on, more than one of my mentors urged me to avoid committees if at all possible. While there were a few exceptions, my experience with such groups over the years has pretty much validated this view.

Too often I've seen these committee exercises result in a thick, almost incomprehensible strategic plan that ends up collecting dust on a shelf. A group discussion of where to go and what to do, a conference where all opinions and ideas are good, a session where nobody can be offended—these most often produce a bland, watered-down product that lacks clarity and punch. The key ingredients may be in there, but are now unidentifiable, like the flour in a cake.

Further, a discussion of "our values" at these retreats usually leads to the same list of nice, feel-good words as every other organization but, later, cannot be quoted by anybody who was there, much less by the rank and file. Who doesn't value "integrity" or "service" or "excellence"?

In the worst case, I sometimes think that the product produced in this manner is often just a tweaked version of what the consultant already produced for someone else. I've seen this happen more than once where several enjoyable days off site with good socialization, nice refreshments, and dozens of flip-chart pages tacked to the walls yielded a generic-looking product with no compelling relevance to the situation in which the organization found itself.

All too often I've seen the product produced in this manner rarely internalized by the public organization. It just doesn't become part of the culture. No, I believe the leader has the sole responsibility to preside over the analysis, develop a viable strategy, and plot the course forward. Of course, input can and should be gathered and counsel taken, but in the end, it must be the leader at the top of the tree pointing the way forward. If there is a larger group, the leader must steer.

This is the essence of vision, one of the five critical dimensions of the transformational leader. I cannot state more emphatically that this responsibility cannot be delegated to a committee or a consultant.

Just about any decent executive can preside over an organization that is satisfied with the status quo, just turning the crank from day to day, producing the same old mediocre results. But the transformational leader can envision a future that is compelling, one that people in the organization will want to be a part of, a vision that has a sense of urgency and the promise of great professional and personal reward. I've already talked about self-esteem and self-worth and the basic human need of leaving a legacy. The leader must shape and communicate a vision that holds the promise of an energized future that feeds those individual needs.

Vision is something we all understand in the arena of sports: win the World Series, win the Super Bowl, win the Stanley Cup. Clearly, everyone associated with such organizations shares and identifies with the vision and sees how they fit in. It doesn't matter if the person is a star player, a backup player, a coach, a trainer, an equipment manager, or administrative staff.

This vision is where they all derive their energy. It gives them purpose, and yes, makes them get up in the morning. Every task accomplished, every action taken, every move made is undertaken with the goal of achieving that vision.

Private-sector businesses have a similarly easy time of looking to the future. Market share, profits, brand recognition, share price, new products, customer satisfaction, and the like all help to define the future for organizations so inclined to think in a big-picture way.

But what about the public-sector leader? The challenge to create a compelling vision is extraordinary, and the ability to do so is the mark of a truly transformational leader. This is not about falling prey to the cliché of the day. It's not about coming up with a catchy slogan or declaring that the organization is now a "team" or a "family." Those things are fine when they happen organically, after measurable or visible success is achieved and is being celebrated. But nobody ever bounced out of bed in the morning because they were excited about the organization's new slogan.

Unfortunately, I think the easiest route to a compelling vision in the public sector is in identifying threats to the organization. Generally, there are threats present, but the typical public employee is oblivious to them. If people begin to understand that work life as they know it is about to pass away, they are far more likely to follow the leader toward the vision of an alternative future. Ultimately, pride in a program or satisfaction with being part of something great will carry the day, but to get an entrenched bureaucracy moving requires creating a sense of urgency.

When the threat isn't there, the leader needs to create a vision of an exciting and energized future that people in the organization will not want to miss out on. If the vision holds the promise of a new and rewarding role, increased job satisfaction, and an enhanced sense of pride and self-worth, there can develop an urgency to sign on and be part of this perceived new venture. If the leader can create and communicate such a vision, transformation of the enterprise can be fueled by such positive energy in spite of the absence of a threat.

In the chapters that follow, I will share with you my experience with both types of transformations. At OGS, there was a very significant threat to the existence of the organization, and it was quite easy to shape a vision of survival. In Arlington County, however, the program wasn't broken and there were no real threats to the department. The vision there had to be based on the promise of a reenergized and rewarding future.

Again, this is not a textbook based on research in the field. I am simply sharing my own experience with you as both a leader and a follower. I know there are exceptions to the committee or team strategic-planning process, but when it does work, I think such success in crafting a useful vision most likely derives from the direct and strong involvement of the leader. A compelling vision must be filled with big ideas, ideas that can rally everyone associated with the organization regardless of rank or role, a vision that can help everyone see just how they fit in. This is the kind of vision that is needed before transformation can be accomplished, and creating and communicating such a vision is what transformational leaders do!

CHAPTER 18

THE WORST OF TIMES

It was late in the afternoon on September 5 when my wife called to let me know her mother had just passed away unexpectedly while visiting in California. The finality of the death of a parent is heartbreaking, and the sense of physical and emotional loss is almost overwhelming. Clearly, it's the worst of times!

At the very moment I hung up the phone, a messenger from the commissioner walked into my office and closed the door behind him. He came to let me know that, on orders from the commissioner, he had just terminated my boss and that I was now in charge. He said the commissioner would meet with me the next day and officially appoint me as head of the design and construction program. As of that moment, I was responsible for a professional staff of over six hundred who were working on more than 1,200 projects with a total value of $1.5 billion.

This may sound like a happy occasion, but this was a position I did not seek and did not want. The commissioner had offered it to me back in January, but I declined the opportunity. Quite frankly the program looked to be a train wreck, and honestly, I was hoping for a leadership position elsewhere in the new administration. This was just not the "parking space" I was looking for. But this time, the commissioner's message was more of a "tell" rather than an "ask." So, the worst of times just got worse! Where oh where was I to start?

In order to decide where we needed to go, I had to understand where we were. Before I could create a meaningful vision, I had to assess the environment to see just how bad things were and try to figure out how to begin to untangle the mess. As the leader, it was up to me to "climb the tree" and look out over the "jungle."

It wasn't hard to see what was happening in the new administration in general. There was an overall theme about making government more business-friendly, and the governor had convened a special group, headed by a prominent business executive, that was tasked with studying the issue of privatization of government services.

Up until this time, there had been four major agencies dedicated to performing design and construction services for New York State projects. This proliferation of redundant programs was confusing and inefficient, and based on recommendations of the incoming governor's transition team, one of the four agencies had been eliminated as soon as the new administration took office.

Now, I didn't have any political "juice" that could help protect my program, but I knew some people within the administration who could shed some light on the future. They shared with me that my program was most likely the next to be eliminated with the work absorbed by the two remaining construction agencies. This would allow for some six hundred civil servants to be shed from the public payroll. More bad news!

It was clear that the threat was immediate. There was no time for a retreat, focus groups, consultants, strategic plan development, and the like. While I did not have access to the decision makers, I knew there were people out there who did. I felt if I could find them and convince them that my program was about to change for the better, they might run interference for a while and give me some breathing room. That became my initial strategy. Bam!

So, during my first week on the job, I invited the leadership of the General Building Contractors (GBC) of New York to meet with me. This powerful statewide organization worked hard in the interests of the construction industry, was a strong advocate for good government, and, I suspected, had access to the highest levels of the administration. A few of their members even knew the governor personally. I understood the leaders of this group to be tough straight-shooters who left little doubt where you stood.

This was an energetic meeting that opened my eyes even wider to the mess I had just inherited. They described my organization as rigid, arbitrary, closed-minded, unfair, and uncooperative, and suggested that a "mercy killing" might be in order. They offered me a litany of complaints about how poorly my organization operated and how their members didn't like working for us at all. I'll never forget their summation: "You are the worst public owner in the State of New York!"

I asked them straight up, "Where should I start?" Their chief complaint was a standard "No Damages for Delay" clause in our contracts that put all of the risk on the contractor. This clause essentially said that no matter what the cause, even a delay that was the fault of the State, the aggrieved contractor was not allowed to file a claim for the extra costs. Seriously?!

I then turned my attention to the major organizations representing those 140 or so consultants who provided professional services to my organization, the American Institute of Architects (AIA) and the American Consulting Engineers Council (ACEC). I knew they were strong advocates for their professions at the state level and, again I suspected, also had a degree of access to the administration.

The bad news continued. Through these meetings, I learned that my program had been very rigid, arbitrary, and difficult to deal with. The leaders of these professions had made suggestions

Out of the Clay

of how to improve things over the years that were brushed off or ignored. One suggestion had been to advertise our consulting opportunities more widely, not just in our internal publication. But we had rejected that suggestion on the grounds that we were exempt from wider publication because we had our own in-house listing. They had also suggested that we solicit "letters of interest" for these consulting opportunities, but we said, "If you keep your current information on file with us, our computer search will find you!" Yep, worse yet!

I then scheduled a series of one-on-one meetings with most of the twelve major client agencies to which we provided service, our customers, so to speak. In some cases the head of that agency's program met with me alone, and in others I met with a group. But in every case, I went by myself and encouraged an open and frank discussion. I asked for specific examples of how we were doing. They were not to hold back, and no topic was off limits. I made it clear that this was not a search for the guilty but a sincere desire on my part to fully understand.

These meetings were as eye-opening as those with the construction, architectural, and engineering organizations. I learned that we were viewed very negatively. Our design projects were almost always late with promised milestone dates usually missed. Our staff was, for the most part, unresponsive, and they often ignored specific client requests. Projects that adhered to the client's scope of work and budget were rare. Contract awards were so slow that low bidders often withdrew, thereby raising the cost of the project. Actual construction was most often late and was frequently of poor quality.

Their biggest complaint was that they never knew how to determine the status of projects "in the works" because there was no central point of control. Unless they got lucky, the bureau or work unit they called would most often refer them to a different unit. Then that one, in turn, would buck them on to yet another one. More than one of these new clients of mine had begun considering other means of getting their work accomplished, even if it meant seeking statutory authority to do it themselves. It appeared that this train wreck of mine had almost no cars left standing on the track!

But after all these meetings, and in spite of all the bad news, I began to see the great opportunity this represented. I knew we had talented and hardworking people on the staff who, I believed, just needed one thing: leadership. I realized that it was, in fact, the composite of poor performance, angry contractors, frustrated consultants, and dissatisfied clients that made this a situation crying out for transformation. What had appeared to be the worst of times began to look like the best of times, as this was the leadership opportunity I had been seeking all along. So, energized by this new paradigm, I set out to take full advantage of it.

It was at this point that a vision of the future materialized for me, and I didn't need a consultant, committee, or off-site retreat to see it:

A future where everybody loved us, clients, contractors, and consultants alike. In this future state, we would be known for on-time, on-budget, high-quality work at a reasonable cost. We would be viewed as fair and reasonable, and people would like to work with us. In fact, they would like us so much that they would advocate on our behalf with the powers that be and help us advance our organization, not eliminate it. I foresaw a staff where all would be doing their best work and were proud of themselves and the things they were accomplishing, both individually and collectively. I could see clearly how this rigid, one-size-fits-all, inefficient, ineffective, unresponsive, and unaccountable bureaucracy could be transformed into a high-performing model of good government!

As the leader, I viewed the creation and communication of this overarching vision as my responsibility. Yes, it would be fleshed out and sharpened over time as I tried things and consulted with many people. On the pages that follow, I'll share with you a bit more of the story of how this unfolded and maybe give you some ideas you can reflect upon.

As the leader of your organization, large or small, it is your responsibility to see what the future can be, your responsibility to

Out of the Clay

create and communicate a vision borne out of the unique circumstances in which you find yourself. This vision must tap into the potential energy and imagination of your people, help them see what the future can be and how they fit in, and give them an exciting reason to get each new day started!

Chapter 19

The Whole Patient

Remember that son of ours who began his college career at West Point? Well, he wasn't there very long before he realized that he wanted to be a doctor, not a general.

So he resigned from the Academy and graduated near the top of his class at Binghamton University. He went on to NYU School of Medicine, where he was elected a member of Alpha Omega Alpha Honor Medical Society, followed by a residency in orthopedic surgery at the Hospital for Special Surgery in New York City.

Always on the lookout for new ideas, I was very taken with a concept to which our son was introduced in medical school, that of "the whole patient." This approach advocated a big-picture view of all aspects of the patient where more than test results and numbers were taken into account.

In my simplified understanding of what I am sure is much more complex, if the patient looks good, feels good, and has no complaints, don't plow ahead with additional tests or treatments just because certain initial test results are a bit off. On the other

Out of the Clay

hand, if a patient doesn't feel well and presents with certain symptoms, it is probably a good idea to keep looking, even if those first tests are negative.

As I contemplated the terrible state of our construction function—late projects, poor quality, unhappy clients, and angry contractors—this "whole patient" concept appeared to hold potential for shaping a vision for the future. Essentially, we were doing lots of things in the name of saving taxpayers' dollars that added up to a very negative contracting environment that was actually costing us more.

Unfair contract requirements, inflexibility, arbitrary interpretation of contract provisions, and the nitpicking negotiation of change orders—all done sincerely in the name of protecting the public interest—in practice added up to a very negative contracting environment, a "sick patient," so to speak. Consequently, many of the good contractors avoided us or bid high, leaving us with poor contractors and brokers doing much of our work. The results were less than desirable.

As I saw the task before me, it was to lead the staff to a "whole patient" vision of our contracting environment. I needed to help them see that, in the long run, the public interest would be better served by bringing quality, competitive firms back to our program than by continuing to squeeze small dollars out of projects through unfair practices.

On the job for about a month, I had the good fortune to be invited to speak at the annual awards dinner of the General Building Contractors of NY. I took this opportunity to outline my vision for a less contentious, more fair, more cooperative contracting environment, an environment where we work as partners rather than adversaries. I concluded my remarks by announcing to the packed ballroom that our "No Damages for Delay" clause, their number-one complaint, was going to be eliminated. Following the spontaneous, thunderous applause, I closed with, "We want you back!"

This clause was just one of many "General Conditions" written into every contract that combined to create this negative contracting environment. In general, ambiguities or conflicts in the contract documents would always be resolved in favor of the State, no matter how arbitrary.

In order to address this situation in a comprehensive manner, I convened a task force comprised of knowledgeable representatives of the General Building Contractors, people from the subcontractor community, and key staff from my organization. I asked them to look at the "whole patient," as it were, and make a complete review of our General Conditions. Their task was to propose a set of revisions that would move us toward the vision of a balanced contracting environment, a public/private partnership of sorts, with fair assignment of risk and responsibility to both parties.

Now, this may look like the type of committee I advised against. But in order to be sure of making progress, I participated directly and had to push back hard against the significant resistance to change prevalent inside my own organization.

The vision I communicated was clear. With risks being more balanced and fair, more quality contractors would be willing to come back to our program and to bid aggressively in an effort to win the work. In the end, our clients, and the public, would be better served with on-time, high-quality, cost-effective projects.

While the task force was working and the message of my "whole patient" vision was starting to spread, there was a good deal of work to do internally. Even where we had some contract provisions that were fair on their face, we had found a way, in the name of protecting the public's money, to employ them in quite an arbitrary and unfair manner.

The negative environment we created was reflected in some two to three hundred dispute hearings annually. The General Conditions allowed an aggrieved contractor to appeal directly to me when conflicts could not be resolved on the project site or at any other level. One of the first hearing requests I received related to our refusal to pay for a $100 water cooler on a $4 million project.

This was clearly a twisted and unreasonable interpretation of the contract documents, and it would have cost more than $100 to conduct the hearing, not to mention the ill will.

I used this example to introduce this "whole patient" vision to our director of construction, Dave Seiffert. My theme was "contractors are not criminals" and are legitimately in business to make money, not to provide the State with free service. I explained my belief that if we are to be successful, we need to work in partnership with the construction community and create a positive contracting climate.

I suggested to Dave that he send this water cooler issue back to the project site to be resolved and then begin traveling the state to bring the message of this new vision to our seventy field offices and job trailers. I asked him to take personal leadership with his people on building a positive relationship with the construction community.

Dave got what I was talking about immediately and agreed with the vision. He understood the situation and knew what had to be done. This highly capable man had never been "given his head" before or a free hand to fix things. Now, released from the stifling paralysis of the bureaucracy, and armed with a clear vision, he was empowered to make his own difference, define his own career, and enhance his own feeling of self-worth.

I then turned my attention to change orders. In construction, changes to the work are inevitable and "change orders" need to be issued to officially modify one or more aspects of the project while it's under construction. A key element of this process is negotiating an appropriate change in cost.

That sounds good, but what I learned is that the people on my staff assigned to negotiate for the State were very hard on the contractor in an effort to save the public's money. They were very skilled at finding what they thought were "fat" or unauthorized costs included by contractors in an effort to pad their proposals. Contractors really did need to "enhance" these proposals to protect themselves from my staff who, very often, refused to compensate a

Part III: Vision   The Whole Patient

contractor for requested costs, some of which were actually substantiated. Some of the arguments were essentially over pennies. Quite a game!

The result was a protracted and bogged-down process. Projects were slowed, payments were delayed, staff time was wasted, and animosity and mistrust grew. As I examined our practices more closely, I felt we really were being unfair.

Real evidence of this gamesmanship came later on when one of our most skilled negotiators had to leave state service. I knew he was an experienced electrician and asked if he were going to get a job in construction. He responded, "I've screwed every contractor in the state. Where can I get a job?!"

Remember the conversation I was having with Dave about the water cooler? Well, once I outlined the vision I had of what our organization could and should be, and explained the important role I saw him playing in achieving that vision, he actually suggested something that made a significant difference with respect to change orders.

At that point, our organization was very archaic in its structure with many, almost autonomous, bureaus and units. One of those entities was the cost-control bureau, where some thirty-five professional staff were involved in all aspects of project costing from the earliest budget estimates through all phases of design and construction. In all things money, they were king. One of those functions was the negotiation of change orders, and it was here that the idea of protecting the public's money by squeezing every nickel out of a contractor was deeply rooted.

Already feeling energized about his new role in the organization, Dave said, "If you really want to make a difference, move the change-order negotiation function to the Division of Construction and put that staff under my (Dave's) direct control." An obviously brilliant idea, I didn't have to think twice. To the dismay of many, we immediately identified four qualified volunteers from the cost-control bureau and moved them under Dave's control. With an eye on the positive contracting environment we were trying to create, we simply tasked them with timely, fair, honest, and cooperative negotiations.

Fueled by this larger vision of fairness, this move was a great success. With contractors expecting reasonable treatment, their efforts to prepare responsible proposals improved. Armed with this new paradigm, my staff was fair and reasonable in return. The backlog of old change orders waiting processing was virtually eliminated and payments were flowing in a timely manner. Contractors liked working with us better and staff enjoyed the less contentious role they were asked to play. On two occasions, contractors called me personally to let me know that my staff had actually added money to their proposals to cover critical items that the contractor had missed. Wow!

This was just one of many transformative changes and improvements that Dave was able to implement because he was empowered to do so. One of the most significant contributions he made was the establishment of a "field-order" contingency allowance inside each contract, which totally streamlined the process of identifying, negotiating, and paying for change orders. This was such a successful initiative, it was widely adopted throughout the industry.

All of this served to reinforce for me the importance and power of having a compelling vision. Without one, the bureaucrats tend to "turn the crank" from day to day with nothing but incremental progress, if any at all. It's just a bunch of people muddling around. But armed with a clear and consistent vision of what the future can look like, and the role each person can play, it can give them all a reason to fully engage and ultimately lead to a powerful transformation.

And the future, it did come very fast. Almost overnight, we became an attractive public owner and more contractors began to compete for our work, including the one I mentioned earlier who swore he never would. Article 15 dispute hearings dropped from two or three hundred per year to only two or three per year! In response, more than one local construction attorney told me facetiously that I was putting the lawyers out of business.

But one of the proudest and most validating moments for me was when the General Building Contractors arranged a series of round-table discussions with us and the other two major construction entities that I had mentioned earlier. The first sessions consisted of us presenting the story of our transformation and the vision that guided it. In the latter sessions, the contractors were asking our sister agencies, "Could you try to do things more like OGS?"

Indeed, there is no denying the power of a compelling vision. In fact, transformation is just not possible without one. And as the leader, it is your job to create this vision, informed by the threats, opportunities, and possibilities faced by your organization. Such a vision must draw a crisp and inspiring picture of a desired future state, one that every employee can hold on to, can see themselves in, and can use as a reference point for everything they do, day after day. You must take every opportunity to breathe life into this vision by communicating it clearly, consistently, and incessantly, at every opportunity. You are the leader, and no one else can do this for you!

Chapter 20

The Draft

As kids, baseball was one of our favorite pastimes. We had no fancy facility, just the corner of a field where the grass was worn down and stumps of what had been small trees still protruded. My left knee still shows the result of having fallen on one of them. In this rural version of a sandlot, we had no baselines or lights, and our backstop was an old piece of wooden snow fence.

But what we lacked in physical facilities, we made up for with imagination. In those days, my family rooted for the old Brooklyn Dodgers, so depending on the day, I may have thought myself to be Pee Wee Reese, Gil Hodges, or maybe even Duke Snider when I got a big hit.

Choosing up sides was a well-worn ritual that started with the tossing of the bat from one team captain to the other. The captains would then alternately grab the bat working hand over hand toward the top until only one could still hold on. That captain would select first from the pool of the dozen or so kids who were

Out of the Clay

going to play that day. Invariably, the better players were picked first and the weaker players were always picked last.

Fast-forward to my experience at OGS, when it became necessary to choose up sides in the design division in a very similar manner. But this time, there were 285 players!

I know I have already mentioned that the organization I inherited was a traditional, bureaucratic hierarchy, quite inflexible, largely unresponsive, and generally unaccountable. The design function was structured in multiple independent units based on professional discipline: architecture, electrical engineering, structural design, mechanical engineering, and many more semiautonomous mini-departments based on technical specialty.

These units were generally uncoordinated. An architect located in Architectural Design would be assigned a project for which they had complete responsibility. Unfortunately, they only had control over their own work and needed to approach all these other disciplines to solicit help in engineering things such as the structural or mechanical systems.

Having no real power over these units, the lead architect had to make deals regarding all aspects of the project, including the project schedule. Consequently, the success of the project depended a great deal on the personal relationships the project leader had cultivated over the years. A well-liked, popular architect could generally get better results than one who was not.

At the top of each of these technical departments was a "principal," who was financially compensated for having authority over a large number of people, but had little responsibility for progression of the work. As the "ranking" professional in each discipline, they were called upon to resolve technical matters but did not have to answer for schedule, budget, or compliance with client needs.

If that wasn't bad enough, matters were made worse by the separate project management office that had responsibility for projects designed by consultant architects and engineers. This decentralization further added to the confusion of our clients as they tried to discern the status of any particular project or program.

I earlier described the unfortunate result of this archaic bureaucratic structure. Suffice it to say here that our clients were very unhappy with pretty much all aspects of how we progressed their work, especially our abysmal 35 percent compliance with project schedules. What private firm could stay in business with performance so poor?

A couple of years before I assumed leadership of the design and construction program, a twelve-member employee project team was set up to study this question of design-schedule compliance. This was part of a statewide initiative on Total Quality Management (TQM) and was intended to identify the root cause of the problem and the best solution.

This team had been working on the issue for the better part of two years, and when my initial client visits made me aware that this was a priority problem, I asked for a briefing on the team's progress. Consistent with the TQM approach, I expected to learn of the one or two root causes of the problem and of a few actions the group thought we could take to resolve it. I was taken aback when the committee listed the twenty-five or so root causes they had identified, along with the pros and cons of some thirty possible solutions. (What did I tell you earlier about committees?) This group was sincere and had worked very hard, but was nowhere closer to improving the timeliness of our design work.

I once heard John Madden, the famous Super Bowl–winning football coach, entertaining TV commentator, and namesake of the popular video game, respond to the question "What makes a great coach?" Madden answered, "The great coaches know what the end looks like!" Is this not vision?

So, at this point, I shared my vision of the future with this committee, a future where we get things done when we say they will be done, where completed projects meet or exceed client expectations, where project costs match what our clients can afford, where clients love to work with us and would think of no other way. This is what the end should look like! Pretty simple!

I then asked each member of the committee, one at a time, to

Out of the Clay

tell me what ONE thing they would do if they could to move the organization toward the vision I had just described. It didn't matter if it sounded crazy or if they could see no way to make it happen. Nothing was off limits. Just one thing each, period!

This turned out to be a catharsis of sorts where the pent-up energy and frustration of the past two years was released. Wow! Freedom to speak directly to the leader who had just described "what the end should look like" and the almost certain knowledge that each of them would play a role. It was clear they wanted to be part of something more, something bigger!

As we went around the table, every single member of the committee proposed exactly the same solution: break down the legacy technical departments and reorganize into multidiscipline project teams devoted to, and designed for, the work of specific client agencies. I think they were shocked when I said, "Okay, let's do it!" And so the radical, worst-to-first transformation of the design division began!

We kept this study group of low- to middle-level professionals pretty much intact as we began what we dubbed "Redesign Design." Initially, we did not include the upper-level senior managers from the top of those autonomous units I mentioned earlier, as they had a vested interest in maintaining the hierarchical structure.

Finally, as the leader of this hoped-for transformation, I took personal responsibility to facilitate the group going forward. As I said before, even if a group is convened, the leader still has the responsibility to lead.

We met aggressively on a weekly basis studying the pros and cons of various arrangements for client-focused work units. As word of our work leaked out to the larger organization, the top managers grew increasingly nervous, while the rank and file began to realize that this was serious. They saw the "boss" directly involved and could sense real change in the offing.

After a number of weeks of work, the group decided on an organizational structure of four primary business units with some minor subunits within. Much to their relief, the top managers were invited to the table and asked to provide leadership for this new configuration. Each would be given a diverse set of in-house professional and technical resources along with full access to the consulting community. They would have authority to deploy those resources as they saw fit to accomplish their clients' agency's program of work, and maybe most importantly, they would be accountable for the results. Clearly a transformation!

Through small and large group meetings, all-staff meetings, and some good old door-to-door selling in the corridors, offices, and drafting rooms, we rolled the plan out to the organization. Just as Deming stresses "constancy of purpose," all of these interactions, large and small, hammered away at one clear statement of vision! It is the presence of a powerful and inspiring vision that creates alignment and guides everyone forward regardless of role. And I'll say it once more, it is the leader's responsibility to create and communicate this vision over, and over, and over again.

For the people who had been directly involved in the planning, and those who followed our work closely, there was a feeling that this was so radical, so transformative that it couldn't really be happening. After all, this archaic departmental structure had been in place before most of us were born. For the designers and supporters of this plan, there was an incredible feeling of excitement, much like a child who gets the "Just what I always wanted!" gift for a birthday. However, for many in the organization there was skepticism: "How could this possibly work?" To them, the structure, policies, and processes were set in stone.

And then there were those who just thought we were crazy. Quite frankly, I didn't know if it would work myself, and I had to keep referring back to the vision for strength. I knew for sure that without such transformative change, this vision could not, and would not, be realized and our legacy would go lacking. Nothing great happens by accident! Increasingly, people became convinced that the survival of our organization was dependent on such a transformation.

Out of the Clay

We now had the plan and everyone knew what it was, but the hard part was just beginning. The 285 or so professional staff in the design division, along with their colleagues in the Office of Project Management, had to be moved out of the functional units and assigned to one of the new business units.

To accomplish this, we conducted what amounted to a mini version of what professional sports calls the "draft." This is where teams in the particular league, in rotation, select from the pool of available players based on an assessment of talent and position played. Our draft was a bit more complicated in that we had to consider more than the professional ability and technical specialty of each person because prior history of working on projects for a particular client agency had to be factored in.

Yes, every discipline had talented "utility players" who could work on almost anything. But other individuals carried with them significant institutional knowledge and technical expertise that could not be lost from certain programs, such as prison design or laboratory work. And then there were a few who didn't have much to offer at all.

So, one afternoon, our team convened for our "draft." In preparation, the walls of the large conference room were covered with an array of multicolor Post-it Notes grouped by the current technical departmental structure. These little squares were of a wide range of colors and bore multiple colors of writing on them. This was a great system to be able to readily identify the employee, the employee's technical discipline, and the client portfolio primarily served by that employee. One of the walls was largely blank, containing only the numbers signifying the new business units and a list of the client agencies that each unit was designated to serve going forward.

The new business unit leaders didn't throw a baseball bat as we did in the sandlot, but they did go through a rotation of sorts similar to a professional draft. As a "player" was selected, his or her Post-it was moved from the old department and placed under the new business unit. There was much discussion of the merits of each employee and the relative value of each to one program or another. More than once, the discussion resulted in a "player" being moved or "traded" from one business unit to another based on the group's judgment on where the organization would gain the best value.

With respect to the weaker "players," these Post-its were placed to one side until everything else was decided. Then, based on the premise that all people are valuable, I asked the leaders to think about in what specific way each of those nonselected individuals could contribute to our efforts and feel part of the team. Once this got rolling, each business unit leader, in turn, stepped up and said things such as, "I could use John to do X" or "Peter works well with Jane, so I could use him to do Y," and so on. Eventually, every person had been selected and was targeted for a very specific purpose or contribution.

I'll talk in later chapters about the great difficulty of rolling this out. But for now, let me just say it was a great success and validated my belief in the power of vision in accomplishing a transformation. And you, the leader, must be in front shaping and communicating the vision and keeping the organization on course to achieve it.

Chapter 21

If It Ain't Broke...

I'm sure you have heard that advice before: "If it ain't broke, don't fix it." I suppose it makes sense in a lot of situations, but not when it comes to transformational leadership. If you are willing to go along with things as they are just because they are adequate or "ain't broke," you are, most likely, going to settle for mediocrity and never realize the full potential of the organization. My advice: If it's broken, fix it. If it's not broken, break it. Blow it up. Reinvent it. In the very rare event that you inherit an already high-performing model of good government, at the very least, find some way to point to a new horizon. Create a compelling vision of a new tomorrow where the organization is even better than before.

In the last few chapters, I described the state of the OGS program that I inherited. It was clearly broken and in need of a transformation. But when I arrived in Arlington County, the Department of Environmental Services was already an excellent organization with no problems apparent to me. In fact, during the interview process with the executive leadership panel, I made a comment about my views on change and one of the members took it as a criticism of the program. Ouch!

But I knew I still needed to do something to shape a new vision to carry us forward or raise us to the next level. Absent any real threat from the outside, I knew any sense of urgency had to be based on creating a desire for people to sign on with some exciting new venture, like when Mom and Dad ask the kids, "Who wants to go to Disney World?" The department wasn't broken, but I knew I had to fix it anyway.

This largest of county departments was so big and complex, for me, trying to understand it was initially like drinking from a fire hose. As you would expect, one of the first things I did was study the organization chart. In doing so, I saw what I felt was a bit like the "fused chicken" in that old TV commercial for a hamburger chain. Further study revealed that there was a reason for that.

The Department of Environmental Services that I inherited had resulted from a prior consolidation of a number of smaller departments. They were groups "fused" together, so to speak. These smaller units were consolidated in the hope of tapping the potential synergy made possible by melding a set of closely related functions. I am sure that the structure probably made complete sense at the time, given the staffing and leadership in place. But by the time I arrived, it didn't look quite right to me.

Clearly the department had all the parts, but my sense was they were not assembled as well as they might! Not all parts are equal, each has a different purpose, and all the parts have to be assembled in just the right manner for optimum performance. Whether it's a vacuum cleaner, an automobile, or an organization, it has to be assembled correctly to get the most out of it.

Sensing that the department was not assembled optimally, I took a copy of the organization chart and color coded like functions: facilities, utilities, operations, transportation, environmental, administrative, and so on. This bore out my suspicions, as the resultant graphic was somewhat a hodgepodge of colors. It looked a bit like one of those multicolored breakfast cereals, with no clear pattern. Some of the orange parts were together, but not all. Some of the green parts were together, but not all, and so on.

Believing it was extremely important for the most efficient and effective operation of the department, I wanted to rationalize the alignment of functions. I proceeded to develop a new chart by doing a bit of cut and paste, bringing all the boxes of like color together in areas of clear purpose.

Of course, I talked with key people along the way and received some invaluable input and good suggestions, without a committee or task force, I might add. Those key people, including the county manager and deputy manager, could see what I was trying to do, and it made sense to them. They were more than happy to participate in this redesign. It only took a few weeks for it to become apparent to me what needed to be done, and this new structure began to take shape.

While working on the graphic analysis, I was also making an assessment of key people and how they might fit in. After all, an organization is actually an assemblage of people, not a collection of lines and boxes. In redrawing the organizational structure, I carefully considered what clarity of purpose I could create for these key leaders who make all the work happen. What role could I shape for each of them that would fire them up and give them a reason to get to work in the morning?

For some, it was added responsibility, autonomy, and visibility. For others, it was a change in reporting relationships where they would no longer "eat at the kids table" but, rather, enjoy a position of higher influence reporting directly to the department head or a deputy. I wanted to create an environment where each of these key people had a clear vision for the future and felt a renewed sense of purpose. As I discussed the possibilities with those affected, I could sense the energy and excitement starting to build, and I knew I was on the right track.

As the reorganization was taking shape, I searched for a way to express the essence of the department. Combined with a meaningful structure, this would constitute a compelling vision that

Out of the Clay

could fuel a transformation. The services provided by the department were both diverse and essential. Clean water coming out of the tap, traffic signals that provided safe intersections, fire apparatus and police vehicles that performed on demand, school buses that safely transported children, trash and leaves removed in a timely manner, well-designed and maintained public facilities such as libraries and community centers, stormwater and wastewater that was collected without harm to precious environmental assets, fire hydrants that worked when called upon, safe streets for vehicles, bicycles, and pedestrians, and on and on.

It became clear that the department was about providing for the health, safety, and welfare of those who lived in, worked in, and visited the county. Virtually no aspect of life in Arlington happened without being touched in some way by Environmental Services.

As we rolled out the reorganization, we talked about the high purpose that the department fulfilled and people at all levels began to see how they, as individuals, fit in. Further, they could see how their unit rolled up into the next one and so on, ultimately up to the department level. They came to understand that literally everything that happened in the county depended on their personal performance and, ultimately, that of our department. The vision was becoming clear and people were energized.

I recently read the inspiring story of the 1936 Olympic Gold Medal eight-oar crew team from the University of Washington, *The Boys in the Boat* by Daniel James Brown. It was a book that chronicled the lives of some of the key participants in this endeavor. It enlightened us on the hard reality of the times, both at home and around the world. And it taught us a great deal about the sport of rowing itself.

I learned that this sport is far more complicated and difficult than I ever thought. The construction of the shell and its working parts is a magnificent mix of art and engineering, and the physical, mental, emotional, and spiritual training of the men in the boat was grueling beyond belief.

But there was one phenomenon that spoke to me with regard to organizations and leadership. The construction of the shell and its working parts is much like our efforts to build and equip a proper organizational structure, and the selection and training of the crew is akin to selecting and training the staff of our organization. In rowing, when you get all of it right and it's working perfectly, the crew finds what they refer to as their "swing," where everything is working flawlessly and the boys in the boat and the boat itself become one.

That's what the leader should strive for in an organization. Just as in crew where simply having a boat, eight oars, eight rowers, and a coxswain will not guarantee success, simply having an organization chart with lots of boxes wired together and filled with people will also not guarantee success. You see, it's not as simple as having all the right parts and people.

For an organization to achieve transformation, if I can borrow from crew, it has to find its "swing" where it has all the parts it needs, but only the parts it needs, arranged in an optimal fashion, staffed with properly trained and equipped people in ideal numbers, all working harmoniously together toward a clear, shared, and compelling vision.

As we moved forward with our reorganization and got all the right parts in the right place, the vision became clearer and people stepped up to their roles with renewed passion and commitment. Understanding of our critical role in the health, safety, welfare, and quality of life of the citizens of the county continued to grow, and we began to find our "swing." There was an energy and an excitement that hadn't been there before. Transformation was underway!

Chapter 22

Four-Minute Mile

Leadership lessons are everywhere!

Many years ago, I was having lunch with a friend of mine who had just been promoted to bureau chief about a week earlier. I wanted to congratulate him on reaching this important career milestone, so I offered to buy him lunch. When I asked how his first week went, he didn't hesitate to say it was terrible. He told me of raised voices, of conflict, of barking orders, of staff pushing back and all manner of confusion and things going wrong. The more he tried to control outcomes, the worse things got. By the time this first week was over, he was exhausted and beside himself about what to do.

But then late that Friday afternoon, his boss invited him to her office to check on how things had gone. She was a very smart, seasoned executive who listened patiently to my friend's tale of woe. During this conversation, he even expressed doubt about whether he could handle the job. He even admitted to her that he wasn't sure he deserved the promotion at all.

Out of the Clay

When my friend finished, this very talented woman began by expressing her continued faith in him. She then explained that he had good people who could get the job done, if he would simply let them. They just needed a leader, not someone to issue commands! She said, "If you want someone to run a four-minute mile, you don't chase them. You give them something to run to!" Is that not a call for vision?

The leadership lesson here is simple, clear, and powerful. Transformational leadership isn't selfish. It's not about barking orders, threatening, chasing, intimidating, or being any of the self-important variations of "the smartest person in the room" that we have all seen. Oh, have we seen them! It's not about being a cheerleader, a slogan writer, or the craftsman of hollow vision statements filled with nice words.

Vision is power, an indispensable component of real leadership.

A few years ago, I was coaching a young executive who had about fifteen years of service. He asked me to review a short paper he had written about an idea he had for a new initiative in this very large public-sector organization with national prominence. He wanted to use this paper to pitch the idea to his superiors. In reviewing his proposal, I thought I could see where he was going, although I had to struggle through many words in order to get there. I still wasn't sure I understood completely.

But after discussing his idea with him for about twenty minutes, I was convinced that he had a great idea that was worthy of consideration by higher offices. I challenged him to take a simple three-by-five card and write his proposal on it. I asked him to think that if this is all the space he had to work with, what would he say. I suggested he put his first piece of writing off to the side where he could later reach back and bring over the words and phrases that would build on and support this statement of essence.

Twenty-four hours later, he sent me his revised write-up, and it was a home run! There it was, right off the bat, the clear and unambiguous "vision" of what he was proposing, how it would work, and what it could accomplish. Within a few short weeks, this proposal was reviewed and approved at the highest levels of his organization, and this young executive found himself with a new level of respect as a leader. I am happy to report that this bright young man now occupies a very nice C-suite position.

It's about creating and communicating a clear and compelling vision that develops organically from the real world in which your organization finds itself. It's about real threats, real opportunities, real limitations, and real potential, not the fluffy one-size-fits-all statements that typically come out of the standard multi-day retreat. Again, it's not about cheerleading or slogans!

It's about giving your people their own heads and helping them see and feel how they fit into this path toward the future. It's about letting them know that you believe in them and in the invaluable role they will play in raising the organization to new heights and achieving a true transformation.

The vision will be compelling when it hits a nerve, where it touches and stimulates that desire we all have for purpose and meaning in life, where it ignites that desire we all have for self-worth. It will become the reason you and the rest of your organization will be energized to start each day, not something to run from but "something to run to."

All of those leaders I mentioned in earlier chapters knew how to do that. John Egan knew how to create visions of what appeared to be almost impossible things, such as the difficult on-time, on-budget rehabilitation of the Patroon Island Bridge or the design and construction of a replacement terminal for Albany County International Airport. These projects required the coordination, cooperation, and dedication of a large and diverse set of organizations and individuals. On these, and many other projects, it was Egan's compelling vision that made the difference. Everyone involved could see themselves as integral parts of exciting undertakings. Clearly, something to run to!

And at Hudson Valley, Joe Bulmer, an avid reader, always

Out of the Clay

stayed a step ahead of everyone and could see what the most important role was for the community college at any point in time. Evolving technology, combined with community and societal needs, informed an ever-changing role for the college and Bulmer kept the institution out in front. Through his articulated vision, everyone could see where they were going and how they fit in.

In Averill Park, Jack Thero brought to the Board of Education the first-ever proposed set of goals for the district. He helped us raise our sights from the day-to-day operation to a larger view of where we wanted to go and what we wanted to be.

Just as in the case of Bulmer, Thero could assess the trends in education, discern the needs and aspirations of the community, and establish a vision of where the enterprise needed to go. He communicated this through a set of specific goals and action plans related to things such as class size for the various grades or performance goals on standardized tests. Everyone knew how they fit in and was motivated by this exciting vision. We all clearly had something to run to!

The transformational leader is the person who can, and must, by whatever means possible, create and consistently communicate this kind of compelling vision. Without it, there will be no transformation!

Part IV

Courage

Chapter 23

I Can't Do That!

Although the observation is quite obvious, I've heard it said that "without fear, there can be no courage."

Like most kids, I was afraid of the usual things: the doctor, the dentist, snakes, spiders, dark places, thunder and lightning, even getting a haircut. As we grow up, we muster the courage to deal with all of this, but new fears often present themselves.

I've read that some people fear public speaking more than death itself. I'm not certain if that's true, but I do know that at the age of seventeen, I was forced to deal with it personally. It all began when I was inducted into the National Honor Society (NHS) in my junior year of high school. This was a complete shock because I was not at the top of my class gradewise. I learned some time later that it was my band teacher who advocated for me because of my dedication, reliability, and leadership in band.

As my class entered our senior year, I was elected vice president of NHS, again a surprise as this was something I did not seek. But it looked like an okay job because I didn't have to do anything, unless, of course, something happened to the president. But what could happen to the president?

As we all know, "senioritis" and spring sometimes combine to make adolescent males do things they might otherwise not do, like skip school, for example. That's right, the president and another classmate played hooky, got caught, and were purged from NHS. The next surprise came when the faculty advisor informed me that, as the new president, I had to give a speech to the entire student body at the upcoming ceremony for that year's inductees. Yikes!

As I recall, our back-and-forth conversation went something like this: "I can't do that!" "You can!" "I can't!" "Yes, you can!" "No, I can't!" "You can! You must! And you will!"

I had some great teachers who made a difference in my life, but my high school English teacher, Miss Jean Tracy, was one of the very best. She first pointed out to me that I was a good writer. I had been earning good grades in composition. She then explained that I would simply write a composition about Honor Society, explaining the four guiding tenets (scholarship, leadership, service, and character), and then practice delivering it orally. She convinced me it was something I could do, and since she was the drama coach as well, I sensed I was in good hands.

So, off I went. I wrote a composition filled with original ideas and worked with Miss Tracy on editing. When it was ready for the oral part, we went to the podium on the auditorium stage and she taught me about dress, posture, eye contact, breathing, articulation, hand gestures, and so on. This is where I learned that the word is "are-inge" not "oar-inge" and some other fine points of the language. Then we practiced, practiced, and practiced some more. Finally, we were ready for prime time.

When the day came, I was scared to death, but had no choice but to proceed. Even though my knees were shaking, I got through it and it was well received. A few weeks later, I had to deliver the speech again at an evening event for parents of the new inductees. By that time I had memorized it and delivered it even more smoothly. Thanks to some great teachers, I was given an opportunity I didn't seek, accomplished something I never thought I could do, and began building a skill that proved critical in my career.

As a sidebar to this story: I had one particular line in that speech that seemed to impress Miss Tracy, and at the time, I don't think I really understood why. I said, "A man must will himself to be that which he ought!" It is a line that has stuck with me throughout my life and has been validated time and again in leadership literature and in my observations of work and of life. In many ways, it's what this book is about: public servants "willing" themselves and shaping themselves into the transformational leaders they aspire to be.

The practical relevance of this story is that leaders must have the courage to be out in front. They must have the courage to stand up in every forum they can and articulate the vision, express the sense of urgency, and creatively paint an inspiring picture of the desired future state. They have to touch the hearts and minds of the people they are trying to lead.

In my work, I made good use of the "all hands" staff meeting where I spoke to a full auditorium of some five to six hundred people. Soon after I was given responsibility for the design and construction program and completed the assessment of the "jungle," as I described it earlier, I convened my first of such meetings. It was just me alone on the stage in front of this large audience with no podium, notes, or supporting cast. The staff could tell it was serious and coming from the heart.

In this first meeting, I outlined the significant threats we were facing as an organization as well as the high level of dissatisfaction our clients and contractors had with us. I described what was likely to happen if we didn't change, and change fast. After creating a real sense of urgency, I talked about my vision for the future and my thoughts at the moment about how we could get there.

Not surprisingly, I got some pushback from a few who didn't believe, or want to believe, what I had to say. Some felt safe in

Out of the Clay

their own little public-sector world and did not want to hear that it could end. One woman even shouted at me, "You are threatening us with our jobs!" I simply explained that this was the environment as I saw it and that I believed maintaining the status quo was certain to end the organization as we know it. I told the group that if the status quo is what they wanted, I would have no part of it. I'd find another job now and the last one of them out the door should "turn out the lights."

Was I scared doing this, standing up telling them a truth they didn't want to hear, and taking some flak for telling it? Yes, scared to death! But it had to be done! That's what leaders do.

Every opportunity—retirement luncheons, formal dinners, award programs, trade association events, and the like—seize those opportunities to get in front, stand up, and lead. While the words and specific message need to be tailored for the particular event, each one becomes an opportunity to fulfill your role as the leader.

People look for their leaders. They want to see them out in front and hear what they have to say. Too many people I have met in public leadership positions hide in their office or delegate communication responsibility to subordinates because they are nervous or scared or afraid of failure. They may have staff meetings with direct reports and rely on information to trickle down, but that won't work. Transformation cannot be achieved with timid leadership. In fact, timid leadership is as good as no leadership at all!

Transformational leadership is not for sissies. Of course you can get training in public speaking and assistance in preparing a presentation, but in the end, it must be you standing out in front communicating the vision of a bright and exciting future. The message must be from your heart to theirs. You need to feel it, believe it, and sell it. You must create a sense of urgency and challenge the status quo! You must have the courage to get out of your comfort zone and lead people out of theirs! Remember what Jean Tracy said to me: "You can and you must!"

Chapter 24

Stop the Car!

Many years ago, the great comedian Bob Newhart had a well-known routine where he played the role of a driving instructor. I think you will appreciate this chapter more if you take a look at the first few minutes of this skit. It's easy to find on the internet.

If you have ever taught someone to drive, you can probably relate. I'm sure your parents can, most likely having taught you. I've been through the experience three times, and although our kids did rather well, there were some dicey moments. Actually, one was a rather harrowing experience, reminiscent of the Newhart skit!

It was a beautiful sunny fall afternoon and I had just finished waxing my nice, new, first-ever BMW. Needing to make a quick trip to the market, I asked our daughter if she would like to drive us. She had been one of the better students in "Dad's Driving School," and I thought this would be a treat for her to drive the new car. Of course, she enthusiastically accepted.

Out of the Clay

So I flipped her the keys, she jumped behind the wheel, and off we go to market. But much like Bob Newhart's fictional Mrs. Webb, we didn't make it very far. As my daughter started to back out of the driveway (there's that backing-out thing again!), she was turning the wheel in the wrong direction and was going to hit the mailbox. I calmly said, "Stop." But rather than stop, she turned the wheel in the opposite direction to make a midcourse correction—overcorrection, as it turned out. I said "STOP" again, but with a little more force. Unfortunately, rather than stop (she always was a determined young woman), she turned the wheel back again and kept moving, at which time I yelled, "STOP THE CAR!"

At that point, she slammed her foot down as hard as she could in an attempt to brake. Unfortunately, what she thought was the brake was actually the accelerator and my new, hot BMW took off with squealing tires at a high rate of speed down the driveway, straight across the road, through our neighbor's shrubbery, skidding to a stop in the middle of his front lawn. There was dust, dirt, grass, stones, bushes, branches, and car parts flying through the air and my daughter burst into tears. At wit's end and needing to take control, I yelled, "GET OUT OF THE CAR!"

So she jumped out of the car and ran into the house, right past her older brother, who was literally lying in the driveway laughing uncontrollably. As I got out of the passenger side and ran around the back to take the wheel, I discovered that the car was still in gear and backing up. It almost ran over me.

Yes, teaching your kid to drive requires courage. Giving up control and turning them loose is a difficult thing to do. In spite of the best instruction and coaching, one never knows what will happen. But it has to be done, unless you want to drive them wherever they need to go—forever.

This is the same courage that you, as the transformational leader, need to have when empowering people in the organization. I recall a period of time in government where "empowerment" was just a buzz word, and few people really did it right.

Real empowerment means giving up direct day-to-day control and turning people loose to accomplish their work and achieve the objectives and vision of the organization. When OGS Commissioner Peter Delaney empowered me as the deputy commissioner responsible for the design and construction program, he simply said, "Go run it. Make your mark. Have fun!" And then he turned me loose.

I, in turn, empowered the people under me, understanding that this is how the organization would receive, and benefit from, the best work of everyone. Once you have mutual respect and a shared, compelling vision, people need to be given the freedom to do their own work in their own way, consistent with that vision. In such an environment, the staff knows they can pursue, be proud of, and take credit for their best work. Organizational success will be celebrated by all. But if the organization fails, it must be the leader who takes responsibility.

Unleashing the ultimate power of the organization lies in that difference between "telling" an employee and "allowing" an employee. If you could possibly think of everything that needed to be done by every employee and direct that it happen, things might be fine. There were points in my career when I tried it that way and it didn't work. But when I figured out that people would rise up to their fullest when they were given the freedom to determine what work to do and how to do it in order to achieve the goals and vision of the organization, the results were amazing.

Think back to Dave, our director of construction at OGS. You will recall that I simply expressed an overall vision of where the construction program had to go and the goals we needed to achieve. Once I knew Dave understood it and bought into it, I empowered him to go and get it done however he saw fit. We collaborated from time to time, making sure things were tracking well, but he and the team he empowered were responsible for the great success of that program.

The organization could absolutely not have attained what it did if I had attempted to call all the shots, tell Dave and his people

Out of the Clay

what to do, as it were. The reality was that these folks were closer to the work, knew it far better than I, and could best decide how to get things done. They were motivated because they knew they would own and be celebrated for what they accomplished, not me.

Similarly, on the design side, once we established the new structure of business units and set the overall goals of what needed to be achieved, the new business unit leaders were empowered much the way that Commissioner Delaney empowered me. Each was given total responsibility for the work of a specific client, enjoyed access to all the resources needed, and was allowed to determine exactly how the program for their unique client would be delivered.

The old procedures manual, filled with inhibiting red tape, was thrown out. Business unit leaders and their chief lieutenants were empowered to do things their own way, and they achieved great success. Success, I might add, that would not have been realized had I not "handed them the keys."

The leader must not be afraid to be less than the smartest person in the room! You are, most likely, surrounded by many people who are smarter than you in a range of areas and filled with good ideas. This is a wonderful situation in which to find yourself, as long as you have the courage to empower them and let them play a meaningful role in building the organization that you envision.

For your organization to reach its ultimate level, everyone in it needs to achieve their own full potential. If we view each person as a little power plant, all of the power plants need to be running at full steam. To accomplish this, people need to be given guidelines, goals, and objectives consistent with the organizational vision, but then given their head, given significant autonomy to move forward and do their jobs as they see fit. Every time you take something out of their hands and do it, direct it, or decide it yourself, you erode that power and the ability to achieve full potential.

The empowerment of subordinates requires great courage on

the part of the leader because things can go wrong, sometimes bigtime wrong. The organization might fail to deliver services, desired performance might fall short, or some major screw-up might happen. There is risk associated with empowering subordinates, and the leader's job is always at risk. But as I mentioned in an earlier chapter, empowerment is the route to the feeling of self-worth of the individual or, as I've described it, the holy grail of transformational leadership.

Consider the old parable of the chicken and pig and the eggs-and-bacon breakfast. Which is more committed? Well, the chicken is simply "involved" by providing the eggs, but the pig is clearly committed, all in, fat in the fire, so to speak.

That's what you as the transformational leader need to be: totally committed, all in. You have to lead, create the vision, help set the guidelines, and so on, but then let go! It takes real courage to know that your fat is in the fire and fully dependent on those you empower and how well you empower them! If they succeed, the entire organization celebrates. If they fail, it's on you!

CHAPTER 25

CAN YOU HANDLE THE TRUTH?

The day was dark and the late-season monsoon rain was pounding hard against the roof and windows of our prefabricated metal building on Long Binh Post, Vietnam. All of the senior officers of the newly formed Engineer Command were gathering for the first monthly briefing of our new boss, Major General John A. B. Dillard.

Engineer Command grew out of what had been formerly known as the United States Army Engineer Construction Agency Vietnam, or USAECAV in acronym speak. Some of us thought of this organization as "Useless Cav" because of what we considered to be the lack of strong leadership at the top. Our commander, Brigadier General Waldorf, wanted no trouble from anyone and had a problem listening to, or taking, advice. He certainly didn't want to hear bad news.

For example, at one staff meeting, I offered what I thought to be a constructive comment on a proposal put forth by the general. The red-faced general responded sternly, "Do you have a problem with this, young captain?!" Suddenly, envisioning a reassignment to the "bush," I replied, "NO SIR! No problem whatsoever, sir!" And from that point on, I kept my mouth shut and my suggestions to myself.

Remember Schofield's definition? This is an example of the kind of leader subordinates hope will fail. It's also a surefire way to make sure you do not get the best out of your people.

But in late 1969, everything changed when the organization took on an expanded mission, becoming responsible for both combat and construction engineers throughout the country. General Dillard was put in charge and the transformation began immediately.

General Dillard was one of those leaders who exhibited strength, confidence, energy, and a highly professional presence. As a graduate of Virginia Military Institute, and a veteran of both World War II and Korea, he garnered our respect immediately. And in contrast to his predecessor, he showed respect for us and listened to everyone regardless of rank. His decisions were clear and well founded and his orders were given in a manner such that we just didn't want to let him down.

This meeting during the monsoon rain was one of our first opportunities to get to know him better. As was the custom, the various field commanders got things started with formal presentations using elaborate charts and graphs. One after the other, they painted a rosy picture of how well things were going in their respective units.

But after listening for a while, General Dillard interrupted and told them that everything he had heard so far was pretty much useless. With all the confidence, gravitas, and charisma one would expect of a two-star general, he began to list all the things that were going wrong in their various units. He had been out in the field and he knew about broken rock crushers, red-lined trucks and other equipment, men and materiel shortages, projects running late, enemy disruptions, and so on.

He demonstrated that he knew everything that was going on and said that, in the future, he wanted a report on the real situation. "Don't tell me what you think I want to hear!" he commanded. "Tell me the truth!" And if I can borrow from that famous movie line, we knew right then and there that General Dillard "could handle the truth"!

He went on, "How can I help you if you don't tell me what you need?" He made it clear that the success of our mission depended on fixing the problems, not running from them or covering them up. We now had a commander who had the courage to not only hear the truth, but to seek it out, good or bad. This wasn't for the purpose of assessing blame but, rather, to use his power, influence, and resources to help get things done.

Engineer Command was, indeed, transformed as it took on a new level of energy and commitment. Under General Dillard's leadership, we were excited about what we were doing and continually looked for ways to contribute. If we had to be in a combat zone, at least we had a leader in whom we could place our complete faith and trust. We were proud to be a part of the new Engineer Command!

Unfortunately, this all came to a sudden and horrible end on May 12, 1970, during that series of military operations known as the Cambodian Incursion. General Dillard was headed to the front lines when his helicopter was hit by enemy machine-gun fire. It exploded in midair and all but one of the eleven souls on board were lost, including my friend and colleague, Captain Bill Booth (West Point '66). Bill was serving as the general's aide-de-camp.

On a recent family visit to the Vietnam Veterans Memorial in Washington DC, as I touched my lost friend's name on the wall as I always do, I was overcome with emotion when I noticed the faces of my own children and grandchildren reflected in the highly polished stone. For the first time, it occurred to me that they would have never been born had I been appointed as Dillard's aide-de-camp, a position I had sought.

Anyway, the most important leadership lesson I took from General Dillard is that the transformational leader needs to have the courage to continually seek the truth, good or bad, and then do something about it. The leader needs to go to the "front lines," as it were, get in the trenches with the troops, and work to learn and understand the whole story, not just the good news.

Getting out there to show support and respect for the staff sounds like fun, but it doesn't always go that way. More often than you might think, trouble awaits in some form and the leader needs to have the willingness and courage to face it. As you make your rounds, you will often encounter organizational conflict, performance failures, contrary opinions, vocal critics, resistance to change, procedural dysfunction, or other intractable problems. Obviously, this represents a risk, and facing all of this takes courage because your people expect you to have the answers and the ability to handle any situation!

This simple leadership lesson was made clear during my first days on active duty when a creative and entertaining instructor at the engineer school asked our class of sixty junior officers, "How many of you are leaders?" After some feeble responses and hilarious repartee, the highly decorated Captain Ron Brown said, "You are all leaders! That little gold or silver bar on your collar says you are. People will automatically look to you for answers and expect you to lead."

The same idea applies in civilian life, except our leadership positions have names rather than visible rank insignia. If you are a bureau chief, by definition, you are a leader. If you are a director, you are a leader. If you are a deputy commissioner, a superintendent, a department head, or a chief, you are a leader and people will look to you for answers. You may not have brass on your collar, but people will expect you to make the tough decisions and have the courage to lead in the face of whatever adversity may arise!

Let me share just one example from my experience in Arlington County. In my own effort to seek the truth and know what was really going on, I went to the scene of another water-main break, much bigger than the one I mentioned in an earlier chapter. During this visit, I unexpectedly ran into several serious problems, including conflict between utilities personnel and our safety chief, some dangerous practices for night work that were a residual of a relatively recent work site fatality, and a significant deficiency in the role of engineering staff during the resolution of such large repair operations.

I found myself in a delicate position, not wanting to take sides or levy criticism, but needing to carefully facilitate the conversation in the face of serious staff conflict. Clearly, it would have been much easier to ignore the situation and go home to dinner. But the opportunity to achieve meaningful improvement in the organization would have been lost.

Over the following weeks, our conversations led to significant staff realignment and protocol revisions without anyone being criticized or losing face. Consequently, the transformation of this piece of the operation was highly effective, and managers, supervisors, and line workers alike were able to take ownership of it.

It would have been a lot easier to stay in my office and hope that subordinates would identify and fix whatever problems were out there. But my responsibility, in the model of General Dillard, was to seek the truth and ensure that issues were resolved. People need to know that you want the truth, that you can handle the truth, and that your leadership will be informed by that truth.

Incredibly, I've seen way too many people in leadership positions who shirk the responsibility that attends their "rank." They revel in the title and accoutrements of office but are unwilling to put themselves in harm's way. You have probably seen it too. But unless the dysfunction is uncovered, the problems identified and resolved, the contrary opinions addressed and the critics met head on, transformation is not possible.

Remember the stories of Joe Bulmer, John Egan, and Jack

Thero. All three spent plenty of time at the front lines of their organizations fearlessly and passionately seeking the truth. They were not afraid to find problems, encounter resistance, or run into criticism. On the contrary, they all understood that discovery of the truth was the first step in moving forward and making the organization stronger.

As a transformational leader, you must have the courage to continually seek the truth about your organization. You have to know what's working and what isn't. Don't surround yourself with "yes people" who will paint pretty pictures and tell you only what they think you want to hear. If you do, transformation will never happen.

Chapter 26

Butter Bars

Do you know the difference between a bar of butter and a butter bar? A bar of butter is something used in cooking. A butter bar is military slang for a newly minted second lieutenant in the US military, a reference to the gold-bar rank insignia worn on their collar. This derogatory term is a reference to what is frequently a complete lack of experience and judgment on the part of these lowest-ranking commissioned officers.

The actions of a pair of these so-called butter bars led to a real test of my courage as a leader. Shortly after my return from Vietnam, I was assigned as the engineer equipment officer in the 464th Engineer Battalion, a unit of the US Army Reserve. The incident occurred during our two-week summer camp at Fort Drum in Upstate New York.

In this position, I was responsible for the battalion's fleet of trucks, jeeps, bulldozers, cranes, loaders, and other pieces of heavy construction equipment. When I arrived at camp, I was pleased to see that our chief warrant officer had the motor pool organized by equipment type in perfect rows worthy of a fine dress parade. During that two-week period, I interacted with the troops and invited them to teach me how to operate almost every piece of equipment in our inventory, including the twenty-ton tractor-trailer rig.

Things were fine until a small engineer company from a New York City–based division arrived with their equipment and was assigned to share our motor pool. They were clearly disorganized, had no visible leadership, and parked their equipment all over the place. In the first few days they had several accidents, including one where a jeep was started while in gear and ran into the metal side of the new equipment shop. The last straw was when I observed two "butter bars" welding on a gasoline tanker in the middle of all the other vehicles and equipment.

To protect the personnel and equipment in my own unit, I arranged for this ragtag bunch to be relocated to a different motor pool down the street, a somewhat less desirable location. On hearing the news of their relocation, their company sergeant came into my office to express his displeasure. He proceeded to bawl me out in front of several members of my staff, and before I could respond, he stormed out of my office, slamming the door behind him.

This is just the kind of thing that can happen when you are out there, and you need to have the courage to respond accordingly. Sergeants just don't bawl out captains, so I chased him through the maintenance shops and into the chain-link enclosure that served as his unit's tool crib. I'll never forget the shock when I found him standing there surrounded by virtually all of the mechanics and drivers from his unit, half of whom could have broken me like a stick. My first thought: "Oh no, what have I done?!"

In my firmest command voice I started, "Don't ever walk away from me when I'm talking to you, Sergeant," leaving no doubt about who was in charge. I then praised him for his leadership in sticking up for his troops. This made him look good in front of them. I went on to calmly explain the reasons for their relocation and told them they could count on my support even after they moved. I reminded them we were, after all, on the same team. We shook hands and I went back to my office.

As my staff offered congratulations on strong leadership, I was able to conceal my shaking knees! Clearly, it would have been easier to stay in my office, but what would that have said about me as a leader?

In civilian roles, even though your "brass" doesn't show, you will still encounter similar circumstances where you need to demonstrate courage, especially when you are out there among your people. Transformation means change, usually big change, and people generally don't like it even if it's good for them, especially in the public sector. Such change disrupts routine, upsets the culture of individual work units, and threatens to undermine the ineffective and inefficient organizational paralysis that gives people their perceived security.

Surely, no matter what you try to do, no matter what outlandish idea you may have, there will be some early adopters who will go with it. But you have to be prepared for the reality that, in the early going, at least, there will be significant opposition and pushback.

Remember the major redesign I led at OGS that I described in earlier chapters? In the end, it was hailed far and wide as a very successful "worst-to-first" transformation, but initially, it was viewed as an unprecedented and unwanted attack on the status quo. It threatened to change all of the structure, process, and policy from which people divined their bearings and drew their security. We had many strong supporters who could see what the future held, but for the most part, opposition was significant and fear ruled the day. Some eight years later, one of our retiring engineers stopped to see me on his last day and actually admitted, "I thought you were crazy and were going to destroy the organization!"

To drive this transformation forward, I had to summon the courage to model General Dillard and my other mentors by getting out in front of the organization and leading. I not only convened "all-hands" staff meetings where I could reiterate the vision and paint the big picture to all, I spent many hours toiling in the vineyards, so to speak, where I literally visited from unit to unit and desk to desk. This was a leadership responsibility not to be delegated to subordinates.

I feel certain that it was my willingness to stick my neck out, my courage in seeking an understanding about how our people really felt, and my sincerity in engaging staff personally that convinced them to give this thing a chance. During these visits, people were invited to speak freely and challenge me, but I had to be ready for the critics, cynics, and naysayers among them who did not yet understand how important this undertaking was. Most of them could not see the dangerous future that was staring us in the face. My job was to help them see.

An example: At one of our all-hands meetings during the early days of this transformation, I made a comment that I envisioned achieving customer service that would "knock their socks off"! I soon heard a rumor that one of our more cynical staff had hung a long pair of red socks from the ceiling over his work station. Rather than hide in the safety of my office, I decided to face my critic eyeball to eyeball.

I learned that he considered our efforts just another "flavor of the month" that would soon pass. I knew he was a good man, and I gave him the respect of listening to him until I fully understood his concerns. Then he listened and learned that I was sincere about leading the organization forward through turbulent waters, and he better understood my vision as to how we should go about it. By the time we finished the conversation, the red socks went from being a symbol of cynicism to one of support.

Was there fear associated with these visits? Sure was! In moving and reorganizing several hundred people simultaneously, in dramatically changing the traditional roles of various staff, and in throwing out the old rule book in which people found security, I was fearful, not so much for my job, but for the jobs of those people in my care. There really was the potential of destroying the organization, especially when there were outside entities bent on doing just that.

These were just a couple of stories (more to follow) about having the courage to directly engage people in uncomfortable situations. If you are out there doing your job as a leader, these circumstances will arise time and time again. Everything I said about respecting and caring for your people notwithstanding, sometimes you just have to push, persuade, direct, or simply get in their face. And if you shy away from such confrontation, if you don't have the courage to stand up and do the messy and difficult work that needs to be done, transformation will not happen.

In the next chapter, I'll talk about a very specific circumstance where courage is needed but is so often lacking in the public sector.

Chapter 27

Changing a Lightbulb

I'm sure you recall my earlier mention of being a helper for my electrician father. Obviously, the "job" was mainly a dollar-an-hour "go-fer," someone to hand him one tool or another or hold the lead light so he could see. But at the age of ten or eleven, this was pretty good money and I thought I looked cool wearing the heavy leather tool belt.

Occasionally, my father would let me perform a task myself. Most were simple hand-tool operations such as connecting an outlet or installing a switch plate. But once in a while, he let me use one of the power tools, such as the big half-inch drill.

One day, he assigned me the simple task of changing a lightbulb that was burned out. Unbeknownst to me, this recessed flood bulb was "frozen" inside the socket. With little room for my sweaty little fingers up in the can, I couldn't get a sufficient hold on the bulb to turn it. I gripped it with my right hand and then with my left hand. I tried every position of my fingers that I could. I even tried gripping it with a piece of sandpaper. But nothing worked.

Out of the Clay

With head hung low, I had to go back and report that I was unable to change the bulb. So my father confidently came to the scene of my failure, climbed the ladder, and with needle-nose pliers in hand, smashed the lightbulb. Yikes! He then inserted the pliers into the base of the broken bulb, opened the blades to apply pressure, and proceeded to turn it out of the socket. Done! Just one of the tricks of the trade!

Think about it. Once in a while, things do need to be broken in order to be fixed. An orthopedic surgeon will sometimes break a bone in order to set it straight, or a carpenter will break out a cracked windowpane in order that it can be replaced!

A number of years ago, during an interview for a position at a major university, the executive to whom I would report alluded to certain deficiencies among key staff that I would need to address. She said she knew it wouldn't be easy and I would probably have to "break china" to get things resolved. Yet another way to put it!

As the transformational public leader, you will be working hard to build your high-performing organization. You will have done everything you can to cultivate mutual respect. Everything you can to create a vision and inspire people to pursue it. Everything you can to empower people to reach their full potential and drive the transformation.

But in spite of all your efforts, you are likely to find a person (or two) who doesn't fit, a person who doesn't understand, doesn't agree, doesn't like you, or otherwise doesn't contribute in any way to the effort, a burned-out bulb, so to speak. Here is where you need to find the courage to break the bulb, or the bone, or the glass, or the china, or whatever, and make the necessary change. Call it what you will, it takes conviction and courage.

As we discussed earlier, this is not always easy in the public sector, and the more entrenched the bureaucrat, the more difficult it usually is. Sometimes people can be counseled out, or encouraged to transfer or retire. Sometimes your superiors in a large agency or department can arrange a transfer of the person to another part of the department where the fit might be better. Once in a while, a well-designed restructuring can help you get the right people in the right place.

But if your goal is an effective transformation, you cannot afford any nonworking parts and you need to have the courage to "break a bulb" or two for the good of the whole. You can't be timid. You can't hide or turn your head. You can't just push the problem aside, which, unfortunately, is all too common in the public sector. For a real transformation, you need to have the willingness and the courage to step up and do this unpleasant work.

My first experience with breaking a bulb occurred a long time ago when I was a first-line supervisor with twenty or so architectural professionals and technicians in my charge. I had working for me, at the time, several brand-new junior architects who were serving a six-month probationary period. One in particular, Lester Adkin, was having a difficult time. In spite of the best coaching and instruction I could give him, his work quality was poor.

Fortunately, the personnel system required that I complete periodic "probationary" reports on each of these new architects. The report was a very simple form that required me to rate the employee as "outstanding," "satisfactory," "needs improvement," or "unsatisfactory" in a series of rubrics such as "quality of work," "quantity of work," "resourcefulness," and so on. Each of these six-week reports gave me the opportunity to recommend that the employee be made permanent, continued on probation, or terminated.

Finding myself at the end of Lester's six-month probationary period, I was faced with the choice of making this young man permanent or terminating him. Yes, this was, in fact, one of those very rare but seldom-used opportunities to screen out someone who was not competent.

I decided that the organization would be best served by termination and got my boss to agree. He did tell me that he had never seen this done before. Anyway, with much trepidation, I sat down privately with Lester and went over the report. I did the best I could to focus on his strengths, tried to help him save face, and described this as a matter of fit, more than incompetence. I felt badly for this kid, did not take letting him go lightly, but felt it was my responsibility to the organization to do so.

After Lester was gone, I was a bit shocked when I received some backlash from some of my other staff. "Why did you do that to poor Lester? He's a nice kid!" So I asked them, "Have you seen his work?" And of course they had. Then, I reminded them of "Dead-Wood Joe" in the corner who had hardly done a lick of work in years and suggested that maybe he should have been terminated on probation. It was an epiphany for them!

This first small termination foretold of things to come. Over the next several years, as supervisor, and later as bureau chief, I oversaw the termination of about a dozen other probationary employees. There were plenty of good people out there looking for work, and it made no sense for us to hold on to the ones who couldn't contribute. It was very encouraging when other supervisors began to follow my lead and look carefully at their own new hires.

It was never easy and always required courage to face the conversations when I let people go. It was certainly not like reality TV. I just couldn't say, "You're fired!" I treated the terminated employee with the utmost respect and did the best I could to help them understand why we were not a fit. Unfortunately, I saw grown men cry and others react with anger.

These terminations were not just for matters of incompetence. Cheating on travel vouchers, misusing State resources, attendance problems, sexual harassment, and alcoholism were all encountered from time to time. The conversations were always unpleasant, and where "progressive discipline" was required, the process to let somebody go was lengthy. Too often I've seen public leaders and managers just look the other way, not wanting to be bothered.

Indeed, this is messy work, and it is natural to want to avoid any type of confrontation and the stress that goes along with it. But the more people in the organization see such things being dealt with in a proper and businesslike manner, the more they will believe that the leader is courageously taking the organization on a path toward transformation.

Remember the "buzz"? Word of cheaters and nonperformers being rooted out of the organization travels fast and helps to build identity and pride! As the culture shifts, greater will become the support and assistance for the courageous leader.

During my tenure on the Board of Education, I saw more than one case of the superintendent having the courage to let someone go because of a serious infraction. In Arlington schools, the assistant superintendent did not turn his head or shy away from dealing properly with wrongdoing. Both men were courageous and faced head on the delicate and difficult work that needed doing. Such action helped build a better team and earned these public leaders enhanced respect.

Some of these people let go were high-level managers. It is critically important to show impartiality in dealing with issues of performance and transgressions regardless of rank or position in the organization. Managers must be held to the same standard as the line workers.

I know this is one of the distasteful parts of leadership, but if you look at your private-sector counterparts, you may find strength and encouragement. A close friend of mine has a brother-in-law who was a high-level executive in a major multinational corporation. There were times he was asked to go to a plant somewhere in the country or the world and close it on short notice. Can you imagine being responsible for letting two thousand people go in one shot? Makes a single public employee here or there look like small potatoes.

If more leaders in the public sector would think like business executives and have the courage to step up and do the messy job of smashing bulbs or breaking china where necessary, the more quickly transformation would be achieved. Certainly, it would be a lot easier for you to turn a blind eye and avoid such difficult situations, but you will not succeed as a leader if you do. Everyone is watching and depending upon you to do it!

Chapter 28

What about the Bricks?

Every other week, I found myself standing in the window of the commissioner's office on the forty-first floor of the Corning Tower watching truck after truck of Albany blue clay being hauled out of an ever-growing hole in the ground. And at every one of these biweekly update meetings, the commissioner would ask me the same thing: "Is all this costing me more money?" And every time, I would calm his fears and assure him that all of this excavation was accounted for in the cost of the project.

Normally, the commissioner would not take such a close interest in an individual project, but this large 2,300 car-parking structure was a major initiative of the new governor. It was located adjacent to the enormous Empire State Plaza, the epicenter of state government, and it had high visibility in the community. It absolutely had to be completed on time and on budget.

The public visibility had its roots in the general community dislike of the plaza itself, the development of which had broken up neighborhoods, displaced hundreds of residents, and created

Out of the Clay

a modernistic stone-and-marble "fortress" in the heart of downtown. Old Albany viewed this edifice as an eyesore that was insensitive to the historic fabric of their neighborhoods. The initial artist's rendering of the proposed garage appeared to promise more of the same, and opposition was swift and strong.

My involvement began with a presentation of the proposed design concept to a gathering of members of the city council, representatives of three historic neighborhood associations, and the rector of the adjacent cathedral. Although civil and respectful, all were quite vocal in expressing their negative view of the project.

The group agreed that there was a parking problem in downtown and 2,300 new spaces could help alleviate it. But what they really didn't like was the proposed design. I listened carefully to their concerns and then explained that this sketch was only a concept. All of the features they didn't like were open to discussion and change. I told them that I would be personally facilitating design meetings and promised seats at the table for their representatives.

Long story short, the design process was a great success. It did begin with loud and contentious sessions, but once the various groups were convinced we were sincere and listening to them, these meetings became very productive. In the end, four significant design features were a direct result of this community input, the most significant being that the facade of the structure would be brick. In this way, the garage would mirror the warm character of the surrounding historic townhomes rather than the stone of the relatively sterile governmental plaza.

In order to stay fully informed on progress, I set up a regular weekly meeting with Jim Dirolf and Mike Singleton, our lead engineers on the project. They were two of our very best, both having excellent engineering judgment and construction management skills. They also understood the need to continue full engagement of the community representatives all the way to the ribbon cutting.

This is an example of how the leader has to sometimes break protocol, get out in front, get dirty hands, and lead where it really matters. This wasn't a process of telling Jim and Mike how to do their jobs; they were way too good for that. But by eliminating the bureaucratic layers between them and me, they knew I was willing to help in any way I could and take the hit if the venture failed.

Understanding how important the look of the garage was to the community, we took the initiative to involve them in the selection of the actual brick that would be used. So, as the warmth of May that year rolled around, the construction team had a series of sample panels put together using various brick-and-mortar combinations. We then gathered a large community group to review the panels and make a selection. After lengthy discussion, the group settled on a nice "Rubigo Red Smooth."

Immediately, our Monday agenda included an item on acquisition of the almost two hundred thousand bricks needed for the project. This was of particular concern because a significant industry-wide brick shortage had developed and lead times were significant. Each week I would ask, "What about the bricks?" And every week Jim and Mike assured me there would be no problem.

After a number of weeks of growing increasingly agitated, I demanded more detail about how these guys could be so calm and feel so confident. We were getting closer to the time the bricks would be needed and I was getting nervous. The schedule was critical and we had no room for failure. So again, "What about the bricks?!"

Finally, Jim saw that I was getting seriously concerned, and he turned to Mike and said, "I think you better tell him." I'll never forget that moment! As the blood drained from my face and I braced for the bad news, I managed to ask, "Tell me what?" After sheepishly hanging his head for a moment, Mike said, "The bricks will be here on time." When I asked how he knew for sure, he said, "We ordered them in February!"

Think about it. They ordered the bricks in February, a full three months before the brick had been selected by the community. They did this because they understood the impact the critical shortage could have had on the project schedule. In the interests

Out of the Clay

of the project, and the organization, these guys took a calculated risk and guessed right. I could not have been more proud!

At my next meeting with the commissioner, as we looked out the window down at the construction, he happened to ask about bricks. He, too, was aware of the shortage. When I told him what had transpired, he just smiled and said, "Bill, you have put together one heck of a team!"

This doesn't sound like typical government work, does it? Most of the time, the bureaucrat won't stick his or her neck out and will use the red tape or procedural paralysis as cover for just plodding along by the numbers. If results are bad, it's the fault of people or things outside their control. In this case, a schedule slippage could be blamed on an unforeseen industry problem.

I was proud of Jim and Mike because they stepped up and assumed responsibility for this project. They were both excellent engineers to start with, but I watched them grow as savvy leaders, leaders who were willing to take risks. They did things that one can't find in the manual in order to carry out their mission and meet their objective.

This is the kind of careful and calculated risk-taking the transformational leader needs to exhibit. But it takes courage! I like to think that it was my own willingness to take risks that inspired these guys to feel comfortable in taking risks themselves. They were confident that I would have their backs and would take responsibility if it went wrong. As I mentioned earlier, it takes courage to empower subordinates. But it takes another whole level of courage to allow them, and actually encourage them, to take risks when necessary. But just imagine the capability of an entire organization of people who are empowered to think for themselves and encouraged to take their own calculated risks. Wow!

Over the years, I have studied and used many of the leadership principles espoused by great scholars such as Covey, Deming, Bennis, Kotter, and others. But when it comes to the issue of risk, the concept that I have found most useful is from Tom Peters: "Ready! Fire! Aim!"

Too often the leader is mired in thinking and planning and planning some more, frozen in a holding pattern, afraid to take action because it might be wrong, afraid of making a mistake, afraid of failure. Pulling the trigger without being fully aimed is risky. But the leader must have the courage to act, to move forward, to take such risks. Otherwise, transformation will not happen! Personally, I think frittering away time with excessive planning is a much greater risk than getting a pretty good idea of what to do and doing it! This approach has worked well for me.

Granted, sometimes your idea or action does not work out. It is then that you must have the courage to admit you're wrong, change direction, or maybe even abandon the idea completely. I certainly have had to make adjustments from time to time to sharpen things up, but overall this commitment to forward motion has yielded significant positive results.

When I began my work as a department head in Arlington County, I had a series of one-on-one meetings with a number of key members of the department. Overall, their guidance was to look around and get to know the place better before making any changes. Ascribing to the "if it ain't broke" principle, two of the most competent members of our team even advised that I shouldn't make any changes for a period of six months.

But that wasn't me or what I believed in. I had seen too many examples of studies and planning that went on for what seemed like forever only to yield mediocre results. Even the most well-thought-out plans needed adjustment in the end anyway, and some didn't work at all. I believe the best time to initiate change is as soon as you can after you assume leadership of an organization. You do need to make some measure of assessment or evaluation, but the longer the status quo continues to get "baked in" on your watch, the harder it will be for you to lead change later.

So contrary to the prevailing advice, I had a reorganization plan (chapter 21) on the county manager's desk within six weeks. I received quick approval and moved ahead immediately. Most of the plan was well received and went into place quite smoothly.

Out of the Clay

Quick adjustments were made to rectify the minor parts that didn't quite work, and people at all levels felt empowered to build out the detail of how to do their own jobs, consistent with the vision.

This phenomenon really energized the implementation, and it resulted in a far more effective organizational design than could have been achieved through months of planning and the preparation of a many-inches-thick detailed plan. Was this risky? Absolutely! Did I need courage? You bet!

Remember the reorganization at OGS I talked about in chapters 19 and 20, the one where we disrupted the archaic organizational structure and moved several hundred people simultaneously? Was this risky? Absolutely! There was so much that could have gone wrong, not the least of which could have been a staff revolt. If it didn't work, I could have lost my job, but worse yet, lost the jobs of everybody in the organization.

It would have been safer for me to sit in my office and let things roll along as they had been. After all, when the organization failed, there would have been many factors and people on which to place blame. But nothing great can be achieved without getting out of one's comfort zone. The leader must have the courage to challenge the status quo, dump all the parts on the floor, look at things with fresh eyes, make the tough decisions, and be willing to take these calculated risks for the good of the organization. Transformation will not happen without risk. And risk demands courage.

I once had a program within my organization that was just not working in spite of herculean efforts by the staff to make it work. I brought in a consultant to help and she quickly identified both process and personnel issues as the root cause.

When the director responsible for this unit balked at accepting the recommendations for change, I formulated a plan to move his whole program to another part of the organization where these changes would be accepted. But before I could pull the trigger on this, the director saw the light and moved ahead with the entirety of the consultant's recommendations, almost as if they were his own.

Of course my proposal to move an entire program was risky,

and I think the executive who currently owned the program did not believe I would take such a big risk. But once it was apparent that I would, indeed, take such a risk, things moved forward and transformation happened.

One day, shortly after the recommended changes were initiated, the consultant came to me privately and said that I reminded her of Captain Kirk of the Starship *Enterprise*. I'm not a Trekkie, so understandably, I was curious. She explained that Captain Kirk had ten rules of leadership, with number ten being something like this: "If necessary, blow up the *Enterprise*!"

True enough! I would much rather risk the enterprise in a quest for transformation than suffer the inescapable stagnation of the status quo. The transformational leader must have the courage to take such risks and empower others to do the same.

Part V

Intuition

Chapter 29

Take a Seat!

Oh my, was it cold! In spite of the bright sun, the wind chill on this January afternoon was about ten below zero, and my drafty old '56 Chevy convertible could hardly keep me warm. It was intercession, and the design studio grades for the fall term were going to be posted today. Normally, I wouldn't worry, but this semester had been a bit unusual. And so it was with great apprehension that I ventured out on this frigid day to travel the five-plus miles to campus.

It was my third year in the School of Architecture and the design project for the term was a new city hall for Pittsfield, Massachusetts. Our work began with an eight-hour sketch problem intended to simulate the testing environment we would later face in taking our state board exams. As a student, I had been an average designer, but my sketch-problem solution for this project was excellent. So, I was off to a good start.

I labored the balance of the semester on developing and refin-

Out of the Clay

ing this concept and was getting favorable feedback from my professor, Donald Mochon. But with only two weeks remaining before the due date, working very late one night, I threw everything I had done in the trash and started over. Genius or sleep deprivation? Who knows.

The look of shock on Professor Mochon's face when he came through our studio the next afternoon was unforgettable. While my classmates were working on final presentations, I was sitting over an almost blank sheet of paper. When he asked me what I was doing, I told him, "I have a better idea!"

I am quite certain he anticipated that I was going to flunk out since design studio carried so much weight. Shaking his head in obvious frustration, he moved on to the next student, who was, most likely, more worthy of his time.

For the next two weeks, I worked harder than ever before, day and night, with little sleep, and little interaction from my professor, I might add. But he must have been watching, at least out of curiosity, because when I turned in my final design with complete drawings and large 3D model, he selected it to be one of the five projects to be presented to the jury as the semester closed. This was an honor, as only the best projects were shown to this panel of visiting architects and faculty. I had never been selected before, and I couldn't wait!

So the big day came and I showed up with a nice shirt and tie, wearing my only sport coat, trying to look as professional as possible. When it was my turn to present, I began to explain how my building was organized and the rationale behind it—something about holding the building up off an open plaza to signify the high position of government and open access to the public—oh yes, there were the three penthouses symbolizing the three branches of city government, and . . .

At that point, only about one or two minutes into my presentation, Professor Mochon, who was standing behind the jury, invited me to sit down. When I explained that I was not finished, he said, "Yes, you are! Please—take a seat!"

So here I was on this frigid day in January racing to campus to see how all this would translate into my grade for the project. I parked my old car and ran the remaining half mile to the Greene Building as fast as I could. Still shivering, I began scanning the list of individual As, Bs and Cs posted under "Year 3."

When I came to my name, my apprehension turned to shock. I had been awarded a very unique grade: A/F! Panicked, I ran up the stairs to Mochon's office on the second floor hoping for an interpretation. Smiling gently, he said, "I thought I would see you today!"

He explained that the A was for my building, as it was one of the very best designs in the class, especially considering I produced it in only two weeks' time. The F was for the fact that I had no idea why it was a good building, not a clue!

He went on to explain that I obviously had great power of intuition and used it in making my design. He said that this would prove very useful going forward if I could learn to combine it with proper analysis and an understanding of how a building plan needs to be organized around its purpose and function. I was reassured when he told me I didn't need to drop out of architecture and enroll in "barber school."

Soon after this experience, working with a graduate assistant late one night, a light came on and I got it! I began to better understand how to identify the various spatial and functional requirements of a building and how to put them together. From that point on, I was able to bring both rational analysis and intuition to my work.

Almost more importantly, beyond the practice of architectural design, I was able to carry this invaluable lesson over to my work as a leader. Numbers are good. Data are helpful. Analysis is essential. Virtually every approach to management and leadership suggests that decision-making should always be supported by such things.

But my experience and observation suggest that "supported" is the operative word, as the best public leaders I have observed

Out of the Clay

have balanced the objective process with a strong dose of intuition. This is where intangibles or things not readily seen in the numbers get factored into decision-making, where you know or understand something without proof or evidence. I have not interviewed a successful public leader yet who hasn't found intuition to be an indispensable tool.

Obviously, intuition is not something that can be taught but something that, I believe, is present in all of us to some degree. What I want to do is encourage you to listen to it, listen to your gut, pay attention to how things feel, in addition to how the numbers add up.

After all your analysis and study of the facts, I want you to think about how this potential decision feels. If it doesn't feel right, it probably isn't. Too often I've seen leaders force a decision based solely on an objective analysis, or on what past practice had been, and ignore that part of their psyche that was telling them to do something else.

On the pages that follow, I'll share some of my own experiences, observations, and decisions regarding the delicate balancing of the objective and subjective dimensions of leadership. As you read them, I ask that you consider those times that your own intuition spoke to you and what you did about it.

Chapter 30

Overdressed for Success

Three-piece suits. Starched white shirts. Colorful silk ties. Wing-tip shoes. This had been my "corporate uniform" from my earliest days at work, all in preparation for a leadership role. But when that first leadership opportunity finally arrived, it didn't quite go the way I expected.

The open position was that of a first-line supervisor responsible for a twelve-member "design squad" in the architectural design section at OGS. This gang had a good number of drafting technicians, akin to blue-collar employees, and a reputation for less than full performance or compliance with the rules. A colleague at the time referred to them as the "shock troops," and honestly, I could see his point.

I was working in the Office of Project Management at the time the opening occurred. Always "dressed for success," I interacted regularly with very professional private-sector architects, engineers, and construction managers and did a fair amount of

Out of the Clay

formal planning, analysis, and report writing. In a matter of a couple of months, I would be awarded my MBA. Although I had never supervised anyone or anything, I thought I was ready.

It is often said that timing is everything, and it certainly looked to be the case here. I had just received notice that I placed first on the recent competitive civil-service examination. And when I expressed interest in the position, the design-division managers said they would love to have me join their staff. They proceeded to prepare a recommendation for promotion.

That's where the trouble started! The director of our program was a tough-as-nails, highly seasoned retired navy captain who understood the reality of first-line, boots-on-the-ground supervision. I think he appreciated my skills in research, writing, planning, and analysis. Maybe he even liked my ties. But consistent with the usual practice, my lack of supervisory experience was, clearly, a deal breaker. He would have no part of making me a supervisor, especially over a group dubbed the "shock troops."

The battle between the old captain and design managers lasted for quite a number of weeks. It turned into a standoff with the captain countering every argument or justification that could be made for my appointment. "He can't do it! The answer is still no!"

Finally, I was unexpectedly summoned early one morning to the office of the equally tough-as-nails assistant director. A smart, confident, and fearless leader in his own right, Eugene L. Halsey Jr. had always reminded me of John Wayne in the manner in which he carried himself. "Come on in and close the door!" he directed. After offering me some coffee, he got right to the point. "So, you think you can do this job?"

"I can do any job you've got," I confidently replied.

Four grueling hours later, after discussing every imaginable topic, he sent me back to my desk and told me to stay there. Within five minutes, I was called to the captain's office. About all he said was, "Gene thinks you can do it!" As was his custom when he wanted to emphasize a point, he directed his right index finger like a gun barrel right between my eyes and said, "I'm putting you in the position on probation, and if you can't cut it, I'll fire you just as fast!" Now there was a vote of confidence!

How and why did Halsey decide to make this recommendation? Most of the time, hiring and staffing decisions are made on the basis of some ideal set of criteria growing out of the specific requirements of the position. Hiring managers usually look for a person who has done A, B, C, D, and so on because that is what the job entails. Experience generally rules!

The captain was absolutely right from this traditional point of view. All of the objective data and observation certainly would suggest that I did not belong in this position. I just wasn't a fit.

I believe the answer lies in Gene Halsey's intuition and his courage to go with it. I don't know what I said, how I said it, or what he saw that suggested to him that I just might be able to do the job. What tweaked his instincts that made him want to give me a chance? Was it my confidence? My pluck? My haircut? I'll never know.

But whatever the reason, it only took me a few weeks to prove his intuition right. Things got off to a great start. Even the seasoned captain admitted that he was highly pleased with my performance, and our relationship did nothing but get better from there. In one rather contentious meeting with the captain and design leadership team, Halsey pointed to me and said, "This is the only guy who knows what's going on down there! His is the only word I trust!"

After several months, another first-line supervisor, who had been appointed at the same time as I, got "reassigned" and his team was added to mine. This made my design squad the largest in the bureau, an indicator that management was pleased with my performance.

This was a key point in my career that put me in line for the management and leadership positions that would follow. If I had been held back at that point, I may never have had the opportunity to achieve the transformative work that was to follow. I and, maybe more importantly, the organization owe it to Gene

Out of the Clay

Halsey's instincts and intuition for giving me the chance to try something for which I did not immediately appear qualified.

Gene Halsey had made his own singular contributions to the organization as a leader, especially through his transformative "Can Do" initiative to control design costs. But his decision to give me a chance laid the groundwork for the major transformation that took place in our program some twenty years later.

Over the years, I have seen, and have been inspired by, similar intuition-influenced leadership on the part of my key mentors and other leaders. A colleague of mine at the community college, for example, said that Joe Bulmer had such powerful intuition that he almost knew what was going to happen before it happened. It seemed to me that John Egan always had the instincts to make the right move at the most opportune time. Jack Thero unfailingly went beyond the numbers to feel the pulse of the teachers, students, and community and factored that into all decisions.

Yes, the typical experience-based hiring process is the way things are usually done. But I believe that, once in a while, it gets in the way of putting the right person in the right job at the right time, a key leadership responsibility. To achieve a transformation, the leader needs to tap the full potential of everyone in the organization. This sometimes means hiring or assigning a person who doesn't appear, at first, to be the right fit using traditional methods. The obvious answer is not always the best answer.

Never forgetting this lesson, and the fact that my career depended on it, I have relied on my own instincts and intuition in making many decisions, assignments, and hires over the years. Again, I ask you to reflect on those times your intuition was speaking to you and how you handled it.

Chapter 31

Listen to the Hum

A number of years ago, I decided to attend a seminar on Total Quality Management. The presenter was an old friend of mine, and I was curious what he would have to offer. He was a senior executive with a local bank and well regarded in the community. During the seminar, he talked about customer service, employee involvement, continuous improvement, and the like. Nothing new!

But then he told a story that truly resonated with me, hit a nerve of sorts. He said that when he was a young man just starting his first job in the banking business, the very seasoned, old president of the bank took him around town to visit the various branches. Before going into the first branch, the president counseled his young charge to do only one thing during these visits: "Listen to the hum!" Startling advice in a business that appears to be all about numbers.

If that's not a directive to employ your intuition, I don't know what is! Look around, watch the people and their interaction, listen to the nature and tenor of their conversations. Look at their work spaces, watch and listen to the customers and see how they are treated. Just absorb and process as much as you can to learn what the place is all about. Is it a happy place? A sad place? A calm place or angry place? There will be plenty of time for numbers later.

That little seminar put into one short sound bite what I had sensed, and had been practicing, all along. I find the process of listening to the hum, as it were, employing one's intuition, is a critical first step in approaching anything new. From something as small as one specific personnel assignment, to the job of assembling a team, all the way to assuming responsibility for an entire organization, intuition is critical. It has been my experience that the skillful employment of intuition in those precious early hours of any undertaking ultimately determines the outcome of the endeavor.

For me, this was no more apparent than when I assumed the position of director of design and construction for the public school system in Arlington, Virginia. I had just labored for more than two frustrating years on an exciting, but quite dysfunctional (by the director's own admission), building program at a not-for-profit. I could not wait to return to the rational structure and important purpose of the public sector where I could positively contribute, make a difference, and improve lives. My prior experience in both public construction and public school governance made this a perfect fit.

The school system was in the early-planning phase of a major new high school project, and it was not going well. Significant differences in design approach had emerged between the Building Level Planning Committee (BLPC) in the school system and the Public Facilities Review Committee (PFRC) at the county level.

Because the county was responsible for funding approval, it was the role of the PFRC to make sure the project conformed to the larger planning vision for the county. The school group, on the other hand, was concerned that the new school meet the needs of students and parents.

As I listened to the hum, as it were, I sensed that both organizations had good, well-meaning people and both groups had valid approaches to the project. But essentially, paralysis had set in, and while meetings of the parties continued, little or no progress was being made. In fact, the principal of the high school considered spending any more of her valuable time attending these meetings as a waste, unless something changed. She had informed my boss, the assistant superintendent for facilities and operations, that she simply would not go!

Having just arrived in this community, I knew nobody and had experienced none of the history. But experience told me that, as is often the case, this was an issue that had to be resolved by leadership on both sides. My first move was to meet with the high school principal, Doris Jackson, because she held one of the most critical leadership positions on the project. I knew we could not achieve success without her. By the time I contacted her, she was so fed up that she didn't even want to meet with me. It took all of my persuasive powers to convince her to squeeze me in for fifteen minutes during her lunch break.

As soon as I walked into her office, I began to "listen to the hum." I had never met this woman before, but as I quietly looked around the room and listened, my instincts quickly told me that she was a class act, an outstanding educator, and an administrator who had only the best of intentions for her students, faculty, parents, and community. As she spoke, I could sense the passion coming through and the certain knowledge that the project was about the kids she loved, not about her. For good reason, she was frustrated with the bureaucracy and the fighting that had stalled this much-needed project. She didn't care if it was an urban school, a suburban school, a tall school, or a short school. She just knew the school was desperately needed!

I was immediately convinced that I was going to be able to

work with this gracious lady and, together, move the project forward. I think her intuition was working in my favor as well since this "fifteen-minute" meeting actually lasted longer than an hour. And the best part was, she actually agreed to attend the next big planning meeting with me. She must have sensed that I might be able to exert the necessary leadership to get the project untracked and agreed to sit by my side at these meetings to help me find my way. Even though we were essentially strangers to each other, I believe we established a basis of mutual trust in that short meeting, each of us relying on our intuition.

I knew the next move should be for me to meet with leadership on the "other side," specifically, Inta Malis, the woman who chaired the review committee at the county level. Honestly, it took me some time to convince my boss and the superintendent to allow me to do this because of whatever the history was and the resultant pervasive mistrust that existed between the parties. They eventually agreed to what I argued was an absolutely critical step in moving forward, but they cautioned me to watch for the double-cross.

Let me digress for a moment and insert the advice here that you should never "go rogue" on your boss. You expect loyalty from your subordinates, and your boss deserves the same. Argue your point until you win or are told, "Enough!" But remember, oftentimes, there are factors or information you do not know, and cannot know, that affects the guidance you are given. Violating this rule is reckless, and you may find yourself swinging in the breeze and never know why. My intuition was screaming at me that I must meet with this woman, but I would not do so unless given clearance.

Okay, back to the story. Admittedly, I was a bit nervous about this meeting because I knew that it could make or break the project. But I was very encouraged by the positive manner in which my suggestion to meet one on one was received.

As I walked into the small coffee shop near the courthouse, Inta was already waiting for me. Again, listening carefully to the hum,

I found her to be much like the principal, very professional, experienced, and serious about her responsibility and passionate about the planning vision and goals for the county. All other information and opinions aside, I prefer to rely on my own intuition because it has rarely let me down. I had no idea what may have happened in the past, but my instincts immediately told me that she was someone I could trust and that we could work together to move the project forward.

As in the case of the principal, I think this woman's instincts told her that things had significantly changed for the better at the school system and that I was someone with whom she could work. I certainly did my best to communicate a sincere and honest desire to make things better and move things forward. I have found that such one-on-one private meetings communicate respect and a willingness to listen and build a foundation for trust. Having nothing else to go on, I think our respective intuition gave us hope that this relationship could work.

I followed these conversations up with similar meetings with the chair of the planning group on the school side as well as the architects for the project. Again, I sensed that these were good people with the right motivation and that I could trust them as well.

It was then, on the basis of the trust established during these first conversations, that together we found common ground and moved the project forward in a highly successful manner. Rather than a contentious, stressful relationship, a sense of oneness developed and the process became an enjoyable experience for all involved. Participants actually began looking forward to meetings and watching the progress as it was being made.

It was with a great sense of pride on the part of all the planners, designers, contractors, and community that the ribbon was ultimately cut and the 1,600 students moved into this beautiful new facility. This school was viewed by all as an asset to both the school system and the county.

This project was an example of how government is supposed

to work. Rather than silos, compartments, turf battles, and petty quests for credit, this group of wonderful people worked together to overcome their differences and accomplish something great. But absent the willingness of the key leadership figures to trust and act on their intuition, the project may have remained in paralysis for many more months or years to come. Leaders who want to make a difference must have intuition and have the courage to act on it. Such leaders have developed the ability to know or understand what is right without proof.

One may ask, what I would have done if my instincts told me that among these key leaders someone had an improper motive or agenda, could not be trusted, or was just not a good fit? In that case, I would search for alternative routes forward, find people who could be trusted, and work to make changes in the team structure. I'll give an example of this in the next chapter.

CHAPTER 32

BEST BATTLE EVER LOST

It was a splendid summer afternoon as we rode on an old, light-gauge rail car taking in a glorious section of forest in the Catskill Mountains. It was a beautiful ride, that is, until we crossed a small bridge, and without warning, the historic little car jumped the track, almost tossing us into the stream below. Realizing we were in the middle of nowhere, we had no alternative but for the dozen or so of us to lift the heavy machinery back on the rails and proceed on our way.

This was just one of a series of adventures that began around 1990, when I found myself in the middle of a conflict between my agency and a distinguished citizens advisory group, convened and led by a prominent member of the State Assembly, Maurice Hinchey. At issue was the design of a new interpretive center for the Catskill Mountain region of New York.

This group did not want my organization, the Office of General Services, to design the project because they believed it would end up looking like "a Rite Aid drugstore in downtown Albany." I guess this view was influenced and, quite frankly, justified by the presence of an old prefabricated metal building that stood adjacent to the proposed interpretive center site. OGS had designed this utilitarian highway equipment shop in years past for the NYS Department of Transportation, and it wasn't exactly a beautiful work of architecture. I certainly couldn't disagree with the committee's view on this and, indeed, would have taken the same position!

After many years of advocacy, Assemblyman Hinchey was finally able to secure a line item in the state budget that would provide funding for a private-sector architectural consultant who would design the project under the careful supervision and guidance of the advisory committee. But at the urging of the Division of Budget, the governor vetoed the line item and the battle lines were drawn. I had no idea why, but the Division of Budget insisted that OGS be responsible for the project, and our design staff quickly began work.

Since this project had high visibility, obvious political implications, and was getting off to a rocky start, the commissioner was concerned about who on my staff would lead the effort. Even though I was at an executive level, and responsible for the entire Division of Design, I told him my instinct was to do it myself. He was quite pleased to hear that.

I knew the right first step would be to go directly to meet with Assemblyman Hinchey, as he was the clear leader and advocate for the proposed center. Without his support, this project wasn't going anyplace! I made an appointment to meet him in his office and arrived right on time wearing my best suit. For me, this meeting had all the stress and apprehension of a job interview, and I guess, on some level, it was.

Although completely professional and respectful, the assemblyman began by expressing anger and clear disappointment with the veto of the line item for which he fought so hard. Actually, I couldn't blame him. As I recall, he intimated that my commissioner had something to do with it, which seemed to make him an even more reluctant customer than he was before. What the background really was I did not know and, to this day, still don't. I just wanted to get to work on the project.

I assured Assemblyman Hinchey that I knew nothing about that and was there just to make a fresh beginning to the project. Once we got by that, I asked him to share with me his expectations and vision for the center, and he then allowed me to tell him about myself, our latest organizational philosophy, and the approach I expected we would take. I assured him of my direct leadership and my personal commitment to making this a project of which he and the advisory committee could be proud.

I had never met this man before, but I liked and respected him immediately, even when he was angry. After all, he was just fighting for what he believed in. My intuition told me he was tough but fair and that I would be able to work with him. Even more importantly, I sensed that he was the kind of transformational leader from whom I could learn a great deal.

Now, Assemblyman Hinchey had no more to go on than I did. Obviously, he had never met me either, and because my organization designed only utilitarian structures, I had no examples of similar work to show him. But in spite of that, he said that our discussion had evoked a strong feeling of confidence and that he looked forward to working together on the project.

What was going on here? We were looking each other in the eye, listening carefully, and relying heavily on instinct in deciding how we would move forward from that point. It was clear that we sensed we could trust each other based pretty much on intuition alone, since there wasn't much else to work with. I'll say it here, and will probably say it again, but intuition is an indispensable tool for the transformational leader! I have yet to meet a successful executive who doesn't rely on it to one degree or another.

The next challenge came when I first met with the citizens advisory committee, most of whom were equally angry that they were stuck with OGS. Attending the meeting with me was Michael, one of our staff architects who had done some preliminary work on the project and was known to the committee.

Out of the Clay

While there was no open hostility expressed whatsoever, "listening to the hum," my gut told me that the committee did not like Michael and had little confidence in him. Worse yet, I sensed that Michael didn't particularly care for them either. Even though he was very talented, actually one of our best, my intuition told me that I needed to make an immediate change, rather than take the old government approach, "This is our guy. Deal with it!"

Just in case I had any doubt about the challenge I faced, one of the advisory committee members cautioned me as this initial meeting broke up: "I'm going to be a real pain in the ass on this thing and you better be ready!" I assured him that I understood that it was his project, and I guaranteed that he would be satisfied in the end. This validated my sense that I had to select staff carefully and put together just the right team to work with me on this important undertaking!

On my return to the office, I didn't waste any time in making the staff switch. I thanked Michael for his work to date, and on some level, he was relieved to be out of this thing. I handpicked Jim Jamieson, the staff architect my intuition told me had the right personality and demeanor to weather what was going to be some rough going. I filled Jim in on the background as I knew it and told him we had some serious relationship building to do before we could make much progress. This act alone sent a strong and positive message to Assemblyman Hinchey and the advisory committee that things were, indeed, going to be different.

We added a landscape architect to the team and entered a period of what we dubbed "human engineering." Over a period of months, we visited many of the iconic sites in the Catskill Mountains in an effort to learn the history of the region. Our goal was to learn the project requirements and fully understand the vision the advisory committee had for the center as a "quintessential Catskills experience."

Accompanied by various members of the committee, we visited the locations of former resorts, we took in views of the reservoirs and fly-fishing creeks, we had lunch in the dining car of an old train, we rode on the ill-fated narrow-gauge rail cart mentioned above, and we even went mountain climbing on one frosty morning in the fall. We climbed trees and went up in a bucket lift to check on potential views. Over this period, we developed strong and trusting relationships with the committee and were able to begin to move the project forward.

As a consequence, the design meetings were very productive. To enhance the process, the committee brought in Alf Evers, the iconic historian for the region, who shared with us some very enriching perspectives and stories of the Catskills. And, much to my surprise, Assemblyman Hinchey attended all of these design sessions in person. He demonstrated himself to be the strong, honest, and visionary leader I thought he was!

In the end, we developed a plan in which we all took pride and unveiled it at a public press conference at Kingston City Hall. In speaking at this event, Assemblyman Hinchey reviewed the history of the project and its development, including his initial strong opposition to OGS. But it was an exciting moment for me and the rest of our team when he said, "OGS knows how to listen! OGS is talented and does high-quality work!" And referring to his earlier attempts to keep us off the project he said, "This was the best battle I ever lost!" As you can imagine, a long career in public service will yield many memorable events. But for me, the pride of this moment is something that time has yet to diminish.

I am certain that if Maurice Hinchey and I had not relied on our intuition, intuition that told us we could trust each other, this project would never have been the success that it was. All of the hard evidence certainly suggested otherwise. Further, the reliance on intuition was critical in selecting just the right people from our talented staff, people who could build productive relationships with the committee. Sometimes, as a leader, you just have to go with your gut!

This project was one of the most rewarding of my career, and I value the relationships that developed, especially with Maurice Hinchey. I spoke with him several times after he was elected to the Congress of the United States, where he continued to employ both his knowledge and instincts on behalf of his constituents, especially on issues of the environment. To this day, I possess and value the original large-scale colored site-plan map that every member of the committee and planning team signed the day we reached agreement on the site design.

Following the Kingston press conference, the site-development phase of the project was undertaken, but unfortunately, political and economic forces combined to halt progress before the building itself could be built. But I am happy to report that, after twenty more years of relentless advocacy by Congressman Hinchey, construction of the center became a reality and the spectacularly beautiful Maurice D. Hinchey Catskills Interpretive Center now adorns the site that had been prepared so many years before. I have since conveyed the original site-plan map to the Center for safekeeping.

CHAPTER 33

WHO, ME?

It was shortly after I assumed responsibility for the design and construction program that one of my key people informed me that he was leaving to accept a position elsewhere. This was a serious blow, as John O'Donnell was one of the very best we had. Clearly, that's why he was "stolen" by another organization and why, after a number of years, he became CEO of that organization.

This loss hit me hard, as I had intended to include John in a significant way as we began to transform the organization. He had been responsible for the consultant-services program, which, as you have already read, was an area critical to my strategy of building advocacy outside our organization. What to do?

As you know, the usual place to look for a replacement is among that group of people already involved in the program. But I was not going to be satisfied with business as usual or with incremental change. Transformation demanded more.

I considered a number of people on the staff, giving as much

Out of the Clay

thought to the intangibles as I did to current duties and experience. I was relying as much on intuition as anything else. I had to find something that felt right!

Eventually, my thoughts turned to Diane McGuirk, and I knew immediately that she was the right person for the job. She had been a loyal contributor to the larger program for many years, but had nothing whatsoever to do with the consultant program.

I invited her to my office and started by mentioning that John was leaving. She responded immediately, "Yes, I know. And I know just the person for the job." Apparently, she thought I was seeking a recommendation from her, just the sort of thing I often did.

But this time, I stopped her short and told her that I already knew who the best person was! I had no idea who she was going to recommend because my intuition was screaming at me that I had the right person in front of me. Her response was, "Who, me?"

We had a wonderful conversation about my vision for the program and the critical role I suspected it was going to play in transforming, and saving, the organization. I explained her personal attributes as I saw them and why I thought she was a perfect fit.

As we talked and exchanged ideas, I could sense her interest grow and her passion being kindled. I really didn't have to twist her arm. If I could have read her mind, I think I could have seen her early ideas on what to do and how to do it. She understood the vision, and all I had to do was turn her loose.

I think it's important to point out that there was no promotion involved here. It was just a chance to grow and develop, and an exciting opportunity to help take the organization to the next level.

Long story short, she accepted the position, and her contributions to that program, and the transformation that followed, exceeded all expectations! The feedback from the private sector was immediate and overwhelmingly positive. We moved from an adversarial relationship to one that included a formal partnering agreement. Along the way, we were recognized with a national award from the private sector for our qualifications-based selection process.

I've said it before, but one of the most critical roles of the leader is getting the right person in the right job at the right time. And in doing this, intuition is an indispensable tool. You must learn to trust it and use it. In the case above, the power of intuition, the ability to sense what a person could do even though they had never done anything like it before, helped put the right person in a position where she could make a singular contribution.

Another example: As an architect, I began my career in the days of drafting boards, T-squares, mechanical pencils, triangles, and a variety of other hand tools with which to make drawings. Measurements were made manually, standards were pulled out of reference manuals, and numbers were crunched in calculators. Drafting technicians labored through hours of tedious hand-drawing of building plans, lettering title blocks, and preparing painfully detailed door, window, hardware, and finish schedules.

But in the late 1980s, a new tool emerged, Computer Aided Design and Drafting (CADD). This new technology promised to automate this process, improve speed and accuracy, integrate the tasks of design analysis and calculations with that of actually making drawings, and eliminate hour upon hour of repetitive drudgery. Of course, it wasn't that simple.

Our first exploration of CADD was done as a joint venture with another state agency, the Facilities Development Corporation (FDC). FDC had access to the technology, while my division at OGS, with a large professional staff and hundreds of projects, was a perfect laboratory in which to try it out. The plan was to house the main computer and one workstation at FDC and the other four workstations at OGS.

To learn what I could about this emerging technology, I made a number of visits to private-sector firms that were in the early stages of employing CADD. Aside from hearing about the technical capabilities of the tool itself, the key takeaway for me was the universal recommendation that I must put the best person I could find in charge of developing the program.

In spite of an earlier consultant recommendation that CADD was not the right tool for us, my intuition was telling me that this

Out of the Clay

thing had to become an integral part of our program, a new way of life, a routine way of doing business. That made the selection of a leader for the program all the more critical.

It's important to note that for me, this meant selecting the best person I could find, not simply the best person available. I'm sure you have noticed that people who are available are that for a reason, and handing them the keys to such an assignment generally dooms the effort to failure. I could not afford a false start.

Obviously, we had no one on the staff with any CADD experience, and I had to rely on intuition, once again. I knew I had picked the right person as soon as I named Jim Davies to head the program. Jim, a well-regarded and talented architect, was the very best first-line supervisor we had at the time. He could always be depended upon to execute every assignment with dedication and excellence. But when I suggested to him that he lead this effort, his reaction was the same as Diane's: "Who, me?"

When I made the announcement, the backlash from some of our staff was immediate and emotional. "What are you doing? Are you crazy? He's your best guy! Why are you going to waste him on this?!" Even my boss asked, "Are you sure you know what you're doing?" My response, "Absolutely!" I had no computer program, scientific algorithm, crystal ball, or Ouija board to prove it, but I knew this was the right thing to do!

We let Jim select a few people to work with him on this project and set them up with their four workstations in our "CADD Lab." As the team learned how the technology functioned, and as they worked on the development of standards, we tried a number of ways to get staff to learn and embrace this new tool. There was much resistance because traditional paper-and-pencil drawings were much faster. I explained to the staff that this was much like learning to play a musical instrument. If they would just to commit to practice, they would get better.

I told them about when my youngest child was learning to play the trumpet. At one point, I went to the music store and sarcastically asked for a copy of "Sick Cows Dying, Book II." The clerk, obviously familiar with all the honking and squealing made by beginners, simply asked, "For trumpet or clarinet?" Some years later, I was proud when I heard this same kid flawlessly perform the very difficult "Carnival of Venice."

Using this analogy, we eventually got a small core of people convinced that the investment would pay off, and we cut them some slack in terms of schedule and fees. They began to share the vision and buy into the program. The ship started to slowly leave the dock!

But there still was much rough water to traverse with many arguments and battles along the way! On one occasion, in an effort to move the pendulum, I selected a very simple project that easily lent itself to this technology and directed that it be done in its entirety using CADD. Staff defied that direction and prepared the drawings the old-fashioned way. To much whining and gnashing of teeth, I sent it back to be done over using CADD.

As I mentioned in an earlier chapter, public employees sometimes feel that it is not altogether necessary to follow direction, especially if they don't agree with it. In this case, they certainly knew they wouldn't be fired for not following such "stupid" direction—and the demands of the schedule would mean I would have to let it go through. Wrong!

I was certain that if we waited until it was easy, convenient, and comfortable for everyone, we would never get there. We'd simply go out of business. My job as the leader, with the help of people like Jim and his team, was to keep that from happening, even if it meant pushing back once in a while.

Fast-forward through the years that followed. The program grew from those simple four workstations with one software package to hundreds of stations on multiple platforms. CADD became the accepted way of doing business, and new hires arrived not only equipped, but expecting to use this tool. Indeed, the "Carnival of Venice" could be heard up and down every corridor. Clearly, the decision to embrace CADD, and the intuition that informed it, literally helped save the organization.

One final example: As a leader, you have probably already

Out of the Clay

learned that change is constant. Just when you think you've got everything in the right place, someone will announce they're moving on and you will be faced with the unexpected need to rejigger things.

Sometimes such a departure is welcomed, as it represents an opportunity to move forward. But in other cases, loss of a key person can pose a serious threat to your transformation. When this happens, I encourage you to think creatively and let your intuition play a role. Turn threat into opportunity.

You will recall the transformation of our construction function at OGS that I described in chapter 19 and the singular role that Dave Seiffert, our director of construction, played in this critical redesign. And so it was a sad day when Dave shared with me his intention to retire. Argh! Things had been going so well! Unable to change his mind, I wondered how I could ever replace him. There were no obvious answers!

I began by looking at every person on the staff at the next level down, and there were many. There were managers of the various business units in the design division and plenty of district and area supervisors within the construction division. Eventually, there was one particular individual who stuck out in my mind who, I thought, could bring a new level of energy and creativity to the position. I was sure he could build on the great work that Dave had done. Remember Jim in the story about the bricks? He was my man, and I invited him to meet with me.

Well, that didn't go as planned! When I asked Jim to consider the job, which would have been a nice promotion, he told me that he was committed to the design side of the mission and was not interested. After patiently listening to me review my thoughts on various possible replacements, and not hearing any mention of the person he had in mind, he asked, "What about Bob Palmer?" Bam! Genius! Great idea! My intuition screamed at me, *This is it!*

It was clear that Jim had been thinking about this. He was as concerned as I about the future of the organization and understood the critical role the director of construction would play in continuing the transformation.

Even though this was obviously a great choice, the problem was going to be in getting it done. First of all, Bob was a structural engineer on the design side and never held any of the various leadership slots in the construction division. Secondly, he was multiple levels down in the organization and far from any line of succession to the director's position. Anyway, the first step was to have a conversation with Bob to check his interest. As you can probably predict by now, his response was, "Who, me?"

But it didn't take much conversation to validate his interest, and as in the cases of Diane and Jim above, I could hear the mental wheels turning already. With the help of the HR office and the Department of Civil Service, we found a way to make the appointment, and we were off and running.

Bob's superior brilliance, extraordinary work ethic, vision, energy, humility, and respect for all people served him well as he was immediately and warmly accepted by everyone in the construction division, including those he jumped over. He quickly picked up the work of his predecessor and led the program to new levels.

He was embraced by the construction contracting community, as they saw him as tough but fair. He was very creative and continually developed or introduced new technologies or better ways of doing things. He built a very effective bridge with the design program, a strong partnership that had been lacking in years past.

Bob's appointment, although totally unsupported by any data or rational decision process, was one of the smartest moves we ever made. He quickly exceeded all expectations. Were it not for the powerful tool of intuition, the organization would have lost out on a great opportunity.

I could share many more stories of appointments, both large and small, that were informed by intuition, but I think the stories of Diane, Jim, and Bob are sufficient to demonstrate the power of this indispensable tool in personnel decisions. There is no doubt in my mind that without it, our organization would have failed.

Chapter 34

More Forks in the Road

In the last chapter, I gave some examples of how intuition can play a major role in the selection of key personnel. Again, if you just follow the time-honored practice of making the obvious pick, informed only by the person's training and experience, you may miss the opportunity to unleash some incredible human potential, potential that can help you drive transformation in your organization.

But personnel selection aside, the transformational leader needs to keep intuition at the ready in every important decision that is to be made. Without mentioning intuition specifically, it was actually an important thread that wound its way through most of the stories I have already shared.

In the last chapter, I explored the critical decision to build a CADD program at OGS and the important role played by intuition. But let's think back now to Chapter 20: The Draft, where I told you the story of the transformation of the design program at OGS. Sure, now it looks easy and an obvious course of action. But at the time, it was not! Far from it! We were in uncharted waters,

Out of the Clay

and I had no crystal ball or algorithm to guide me in my interaction with the employee committee that had been working for two years trying to improve schedule compliance.

You will recall their extensive analysis, the mountainous pile of information they had amassed, and their lengthy list of recommendations. Why did I decide to reduce all of this to one simple choice from each of them? Why did I feel that this would lead to a way forward? And when they all chose the formation of client-focused work groups as their preferred choice, why did I go with it? Why was I willing to risk the organization by essentially re-shuffling some 285 people simultaneously? Plain and simple, intuition! I just had an overwhelming sense that this would lead to transformative change, and it did!

And remember my instruction on how to "change a lightbulb"? Those cases where I chose to remove, replace, or reassign key people were all fueled largely by intuition. As a leader, you need to figure out who is with you and who is against you, because no matter how hard you try, not everyone will be on your side. No surprise, many people just cannot embrace change. I have found that if you look them in the eye, you will usually know.

Let's back up further to Chapter 18: The Worst of Times, and the strategy I chose to follow immediately after taking over the design and construction program. The only thing I knew for sure was that the program was at risk of being eliminated. Why did I think I would be able to develop advocates for our program from outside the organization? And what made me believe that these advocates could actually impact decisions made at the highest level of state government? Was there an instruction manual? Had I ever done this before? Did anybody show up to tell me this was a good idea? No! It was intuition! Again, I just had an overwhelming sense that this would work, and it did!

You may recall that one of the early steps in the design and construction transformation was reassigning several cost estimators directly to the construction program. My intuition suggested to me that this move would go well beyond the mechanical process of settling change orders and send a message to the entire organization that things were changing, and changing big time.

The Bureau of Cost Control had been like a sacred cow, and taking people away from it certainly got attention. This move showed that nothing was above being moved or changed or impacted in some way and that people who embraced such change, such as our director of construction, would be rewarded with greater opportunity. Why did I think this would work? Again, intuition!

When I took over the department in Arlington County, I spent a good deal of time working the street, so to speak, getting out there where people could see me and talk with me. You may recall that I personally solicited suggestions for improvements from rank-and-file employees and started bringing people to my office to recognize and celebrate them when they were being promoted. Why? My intuition suggested that this would start people talking in a positive way (remember "the buzz") and get them energized about real change in the department. Again, no leadership position comes with an instruction manual, and you have to find your way. Intuition can be one of your most powerful guides, a touchstone of sorts!

As the leader, you don't have to have all the ideas, identify every issue, or find and solve every problem. But you do need to be ready to react to everything and anything that comes your way. Sometimes issues brought to you by subordinates will take you to where you've never been and be difficult to navigate.

There was an occasion where, for better efficiency and coordination, I had merged a pair of somewhat redundant programs. And rather than choose one of the incumbent program leaders over the other, I decided to experiment by having them co-lead the consolidated function. I felt each of them had something of value to contribute. This worked for a while, but eventually, they arrived at a key philosophical difference that they could not resolve on their own. Both felt strongly and neither would compromise.

Bringing the matter to me, they each made the case for where they wanted to take the program. In the process, one of them even

Out of the Clay

demanded that I render an opinion on this immediately, even though it was something highly technical and about which I knew very little. When I explained that I did not have an opinion yet, he insisted, "You have to have an opinion!" So I was forced to make a decision and had nothing much to work with but my intuition. As we discussed the matter, I looked each of them in the eye and, after careful thought, made a decision as to which of these individuals was a better fit to lead the program. The other one quit!

The specifics of this conflict don't matter. The point is, you must have your intuition at the ready and be willing to use it! Fortunately, my intuition served me well once again, as this program under the new leader was a great success.

On the other hand, subordinates sometimes create forks in the road, or decision points, that are relatively easy to navigate because the choice of direction is intuitively obvious. Over the years, subordinates have suggested many ideas. Some were as small as buying a piece of equipment to aid utility workers, while others were larger, such as a suggestion to acquire new software packages or cutting-edge technology to help in engineering analysis or construction management. It was even a subordinate's idea that we pursue ISO 9000 certification as a quality organization. The leader does not have to have all the ideas!

The faint-of-heart leader or overanalytical manager may find trouble moving swiftly on even the easiest of matters. But transformation demands courageous change and action. In this environment, intuition becomes an indispensable tool!

Your intuition can also protect you from going in the wrong direction, even when something appears to be the clear choice. I once was approached by a search firm regarding an executive position at a major university. The portfolio for this job was filled with every possible aspect of facilities management, operations, design, construction, student housing, and real estate. What an exciting leadership opportunity!

The person to whom I would report appeared to be a top-tier executive in his own right, which promised an opportunity for me to continue to learn and grow. I went through multiple rounds of interviews with him, his boss, the search consultant, and even the wife of the university president.

Finally, the job offer came and the compensation package was well beyond what had been advertised initially. I couldn't believe it! It was an awesome leadership opportunity, and I knew I couldn't look myself in the mirror if I turned it down. So, I accepted the position.

Following my acceptance, I was invited back to the university, where the boss set up individual meetings with my three soon-to-be direct reports and their key subordinates. Each had prepared briefing books, and these meetings were both informative and energizing. I couldn't wait to get started! I really liked these people and the work they were doing.

But when I joined my boss and direct reports for lunch in an executive dining room, something happened. Everything was cordial and there were no contentious issues, but I just didn't like the feel of it. My intuition was screaming at me that things were not as they seemed, and I had an overwhelming desire to bolt out of the room.

As we walked across campus following lunch, I had the strong urge to disappear down a side street. I couldn't put my finger on it then, and I still can't tell you today just what it was. But I knew something wasn't right! Much to the astonishment of the boss, the incredible frustration of the search consultant, and the disappointment of my family, I withdrew my acceptance and turned the job down.

Many years later, I was in a meeting with a private architect and he made casual mention that he had done some work at this particular institution. When I told him about my experience there, he reacted without hesitation, "Turning that job down could be the best decision you ever made!" As we talked more, I learned that one of those would-have-been direct reports now worked for a construction company with which I had contacts.

I was able to connect with her over lunch, at which time she

Out of the Clay

said, "Boy oh boy, did you ever dodge a bullet! Withdrawing from that position was probably the smartest move you ever made!" She went on to describe in great detail the boss, the culture, the conflict, the unrealistic expectations, and how the job was just impossible to do. The person who finally did accept the position was fired in a short period of time. It certainly appears that my intuition had saved me!

Before I leave the topic of intuition, I would like to share one example from outside my world of work. As I've said, lessons can be found everywhere if you look.

Consider the story of the 1973 Triple Crown winner, Secretariat, who set track records in both the Kentucky Derby and Preakness. With only two weeks remaining to the Belmont, the accepted practice among trainers was to limit their horses to light workouts.

But somehow, Secretariat's trainer, Lucien Laurin, decided to ignore conventional wisdom. In the 2010 film *Secretariat*, Laurin advises the horse's owner, "My instincts are to work him hard." And that he did!

The racing community thought he had lost his mind and that he was going to ruin the horse. But when it was over, Secretariat had won the Belmont by a commanding thirty-one lengths, the longest lead in the history of the race, and a track record that still stands today!

It had to be intuition that informed this unorthodox decision. Laurin couldn't talk to the horse and ask him how he would prefer to spend the time preparing, and there weren't any diagnostic tools. The most powerful thing he had available was just plain human intuition.

Yes, intuition is an indispensable tool for a transformational leader. You will continually come to forks in the road, decision points where you need to choose one course or the other. Whether or not you have data or objective information available, I suggest you also tap your intuition for guidance. What fork are your instincts telling you to take?

… PART VI

CREDIBILITY

Chapter 35

Ahead of My Time

I had spent hours preparing what I thought was the most detailed and compelling case for why I should be the new assistant director of the Design and Construction Group. The incumbent had accepted a position elsewhere, and I felt I was the right person for the job. I was chomping at the bit to take on this responsibility. After submitting my letter of interest to the director, I sat back and waited . . . and waited . . . and waited some more.

Finally, I could wait no longer and placed a call to the director to ask if he had received my letter and if he had any questions. I was encouraged that he took my call. Unfortunately, I did not receive a warm and fuzzy response. If fact, I got a pretty good chewing out, as only a thirty-year navy officer could deliver—that's right, the same old captain I mentioned in chapter 30. In a word, he described my interest in this position as "presumptuous!"

Now before you think ill of this man, I need to tell you that, at that point, I had only two years working for the organization and was but one notch up from the entry-level position where I had started. And here I was thinking I was qualified to be number two in the entire seven-hundred-plus-person organization!

How did I think the senior-level people with professional credentials and twenty or thirty years' experience would respond to my "leadership"? How did I think I could handle the internal and external politics having no knowledge or experience with either? Further, I had zero experience in budgeting, public policy, labor relations, or human resources—just to name a few. I had no professional license but wanted to help lead an organization that had several hundred professional architects and engineers. What was I thinking? I guess I was a millennial among baby boomers, a bit ahead of my time. Joke!

I shared with you in the preface that I have learned from doing some things right and some things wrong. This stunt would prove to be about the dumbest thing I would ever do throughout my career. At that early point, I did not yet understand that the leader, in order to be believable, needs to have the requisite credentials in some combination of education, training, licensure, certification, relevant experience, or expertise. Followers need to see their leaders as competent. Again, this is not rocket science!

It doesn't matter exactly what this combination is, as it will vary widely from person to person and organization to organization. Educational credentials, especially advanced degrees, are a good place to start, and I encourage you to achieve as much as you can in this regard. The rigors of high-level academic study say a lot about a person's intelligence and work ethic. Further, I can't emphasize enough the benefit of continuing education, as it prevents obsolescence and helps maintain credibility.

Adding to this formal education by attaining additional credentials relevant to your field of endeavor, such as professional licenses or certifications, will strengthen your credibility further. Without such field-relevant credentials, your ability to lead may be limited.

Just before I entered military service, the last state architect retired and was replaced by an administrative director. This was a man who had been groomed in powerful offices to take on key leadership roles in state government. I was very impressed with him and thought he was just the kind of business-savvy leader the organization needed. But, I was off to the army.

When I returned from active duty twenty-seven months later, I was disappointed to find that this gentleman was uniformly disliked by the professional staff for one simple reason: he was not one of them. Even though he was a superb administrator in every way, he was not a registered architect or professional engineer, and he just could not gain cooperation or support. Just this one simple factor stood in the way of his gaining credibility, and he simply could not make a difference.

After a short period of governance by committee, the retired navy captain mentioned above was recruited to become director, and there was a collective sigh of relief. He was a professional engineer. He was one of them.

Formal education and professional credentials are a good start, but you have to have done something with them. They are simply indicators of potential. Actual work experience and, maybe even more importantly, specific accomplishments are key to establishing credibility. Even though you may want to zoom right to the top, it is essential to make some stops along the way. You have to take on a job, do it for a period of time, and prove you can make a difference before moving on to the next one.

The more difficult these stops and the more successful you are at fixing things, the more credible you will be in your leadership role. As I moved up in the organization, I developed an ever-growing portfolio of stories about accomplishments I made along the way, all of which increased my credibility as a leader.

Don't forget, we're talking about transformational leaders, not someone who will simply occupy a desk and just keep turning the crank from day to day. Remember that "buzz" we talked about earlier? You create or add to that buzz at each stop and it comes with you, or sometimes precedes you, to your new position. People will ask, "Who is this person? Where are they coming from?

Out of the Clay

What has he or she accomplished?" ... and so on. The answers to all of these questions figure into your credibility as a leader. Will your subordinates see you as believable? Will you have credibility?

I want to emphasize again that the particular formula by which an individual leader will garner credibility of credentials varies greatly. I have seen people with modest formal education, like John Egan in chapter 11, rise to be worshiped by their subordinates and lead true transformations, all based on a singular record of accomplishment. I have seen others, like Dr. Joe Bulmer in chapter 10, who built an important career in one field of scientific research, make a superb transition to public leadership. As I mentioned earlier, appointments do not have to be a one-to-one match, duties to experience, but there must be something to make selections credible.

On the other hand, I have seen a few people with long and impressive résumés who have turned out to be morons, like the "knucklehead" also referenced in chapter 10! So don't think there is anything automatic about one degree or another or one job or another. It all just needs to add up to credibility of credentials, because followers want leaders who are competent.

Clearly, I was a bit ahead of my time in applying for the assistant director position when I did. I would have had no credibility in the position at all and would have been completely ineffective in that role. Thankfully, no one gave me the chance to try. When I ultimately did rise to that position some twenty years later, it was only after additional education and certification and many difficult stops and accomplishments along the way.

Many years later, I didn't feel so dumb about my ill-advised application for the assistant director position when a headhunter, who was searching for a new CEO for a major rail operation, told me of an applicant whose primary qualification was an elaborate model-train setup in his basement. How much credibility do you suppose he would have had?

On the other hand, having credibility doesn't mean that you

should take on whatever is offered. You need to be self-aware and understand where you are qualified and where you are not. There was an occasion where I applied for what was an exciting building-expansion program in a rapidly growing public school system. The interview was a home run, and I was offered the position.

But during the interview, I learned more about the situation in the district and the expectations of the leadership. I knew there was no way I could accomplish their objectives, and I turned down the offer when it came. Had I accepted, it would have been only a short time before it was apparent that I was not a good fit, and whatever credibility I had would have evaporated.

I know that many of you are anxious to get to the top and be the leader. I know I certainly was. But don't get ahead of your time. I just encourage you to be patient, continue your education, and work on building a solid record of accomplishment along the way. Leadership can be practiced in the smallest of units and built on from there. How you do it can and will vary widely, but without solid credentials, you will not be believable and will not be able to take on the difficult work of leading a transformation.

Chapter 36

Doctor George

I'm sure you will recall the earlier chapter where I described my "near-death" experience with the mandatory statistics course that led off my MBA program. I still don't know how I ever got through it. But happily, it was followed by one of my favorite courses ever, Organizational Behavior.

This course was very interesting and addressed the kind of human-dimension topics I was anxious to learn about. It was a pleasure to immerse myself into the coursework, and even the exams and projects were fun. But the best part of this class had to be the professor, Doctor George. He was full of energy, very dynamic, and hilariously entertaining. I think he was a native of Texas. I can still remember the first night when the class was assembled and we heard him clomping down the hall in his cowboy boots. He entered the classroom with a bang, and with his cool Texas drawl, he had our full attention immediately.

Like most professors at schools of higher learning, Doctor

Out of the Clay

George was a researcher as well as a teacher. In fact, I think teaching actually took a back seat to the research, which is what made him so informative, interesting, and dynamic. Over his many years of studying all types and sizes of organizations, he came to observe and understand what he considered certain truths.

Some of these truths were rather facetious, e.g. "In every organization, large and small, public or private, the losers tend to migrate to the personnel department." While that did, unfortunately, match with my own limited observations at that point in time, over the years, I have found that particular "truth" not to be the case. Indeed, I have met some extraordinarily talented and dedicated human resources professionals at all levels of government. I've been fortunate to count some of them among my most valued and trusted colleagues.

Another observation had to do with the age profile in organizations. This led to his advice that, if you are just starting out and aspire to a leadership role, look for an organization where the current top leaders are in their mid- to upper forties. As you gain in knowledge, skills, and abilities, you will be able to advance as they move up and out. I'm sure there are exceptions, but in my experience, I found this to be the case.

But there was one observation that Dr. George made that rang true for me at the time and has been continually validated by my own observations throughout my career. That truth is, "The people who rise to become successful leaders at the top of their organizations are generally those who display three things: energy, optimism, and presence." Clearly, leaders who transform and reinvent organizations must possess these characteristics in order to be credible. I have seen no exceptions!

Take a look at your own experience and the leaders you have met. Have you ever seen an inspiring leader moping around, looking dejected, brooding, or sulking? Have you ever seen an inspiring leader who spends time complaining about all that goes wrong or that he has so much to do he doesn't know where to start? Have you ever been inspired by a leader who is tired all the time and looks it? Would you have any interest in following someone who is so low energy that he or she struggles to get through the day? Of course not!

We are inspired by our leaders who are always charged up ready to go. They are among the first ones in and the last ones out. They seem to be everywhere all the time and are unfazed by whatever happens. Their energy picks up and excites everyone around them. I don't mean that they need to be yelling and shouting like a cheerleader. But they are ever-present and ready for action, more like that fuzzy animal in the commercial that never stops banging the drum: *boom, boom, boom, boom* . . .

And then there is that iconic piece of children's literature, *The Little Engine That Could*, a story designed to teach children the value of optimism and hard work. Transformational leaders need to be little engines that can, little engines that will, little engines that must! They are sure of where they are going and confident they are going to get there, undaunted by obstacles they find in their way. No one wants to follow a gloomy-faced, down-in-the-mouth person who is unsure of the future, afraid of failure, or even confident that things will go wrong.

I was chatting with a friend the other day who had spent some time in Ireland. He commented on the automatic bleak response the Irish seemed to have when you offered, "Beautiful day today." He said this was usually met with, "Aye, but it will probably be bad tomorrow." Transformations are hard work and risky, but the transformational leader is one who exudes optimism and confidence that all will work out just fine. In fact, such leaders radiate their belief that today is great and tomorrow will be better yet.

The last of Doctor George's markers is presence and, without a doubt, is the most difficult to define. When one walks into a wedding reception, it's easy to spot the bride because she has a presence, most often defined by her white dress. In a gathering of military people, it's easy to spot the ranking officer, who has a presence generally defined by the adornment of ribbons, patches, badges, and insignia.

But beyond the obvious, the bride and the ranking officer usually exhibit other traits that convey a sense of presence to those around them. Okay, for the bride, the dress may be most of the story, but the extra special work on the hair, the way she walks, the grace, the glow, attention given by others, all of it adds up to a presence.

For the ranking officer, it's more than the brass: preciseness of the uniform, posture, grooming, deportment, carriage, pace, manner of speaking, physical fitness, self-confidence. All of these things can contribute to presence.

My observation has been that, contrary to what one would expect, size doesn't matter. I have seen very large leaders who come across as lummoxes, leaders in name only. They just stand around looking goofy. On the other hand, I have seen people of small stature who, brilliant as the morning star, exude an undeniable presence.

It's not unlike the difference between the warm-up act at a concert and the main event. When the star hits the stage, there's a presence that is clear. At a conference, or commencement, when the specially invited keynote speaker rises to the podium, there is a presence.

While not worthy of the red carpet, I believe I have had a presence. More than one person has told me that, and often in group settings I could sense it. Watch the eyes in the room. Do they go to you? I'm not a psychologist, so I can't say for sure how you can create presence for yourself. Without a doubt it will vary widely from one person to another. But I can share a few things that I think have worked for me, some intentional, others by accident.

I have found that staying physically fit is important. I did some modest running in high school and college but didn't really run seriously until my late thirties. I eventually worked my way up to 5K and 10K races, several half marathons, and eventually completed seven marathons. This was great for my physical health, but it also had a mental and emotional component. I believe it has contributed to the energy and optimism dimensions mentioned above. So I encourage you to undertake an activity to improve or maintain physical fitness: run, walk, lift, swim, bike, or whatever works for you. Just do something.

As I got older and moved up in positions of leadership, I began to sense that people looked at me in a different way. "Did you hear what the boss did?" Often, when I meet someone I haven't seen for a long time, their first question is, "Are you still running?" I think, quite by accident, my fitness program contributed to presence.

The fitness component is related to how I tried to carry myself. I always tried to stand erect, stomach in, chest out, and walk with purpose. I considered dress important. Nicely tailored suits, crisp shirts, and snappy ties were my typical work clothes. For many, the simple gift of a shirt or tie is something to be joked about. For me they were always gold. Shiny, executive-looking shoes were a must. All of this was likely a carryover from my military experience, but I am certain it contributed to presence.

There is no doubt that good grooming is important and contributes to credibility. While our young son, Greg, gained credibility as a hockey player with stripes and his jersey number 9 shaved into the sides of his head, I doubt a superintendent sporting the district logo in a similar fashion would fare very well on back-to-school night.

I think you can work on these things and improve through practice. Do you look people in the eye? Do you speak with clarity and confidence? Do you stay calm under pressure? Do you have a firm handshake but a warm and welcoming smile? Do you leave any doubt as to who is in charge? Do your energy, passion, and confidence come through when you speak? What does your body language say?

I will say again that I have not seen any exceptions to this "universal truth" offered by Doctor George. I concur that energy, optimism, and presence are essential components of the transformational leader's credibility, and you need to be certain that you exhibit all three.

Chapter 37

Junk in the Trunk

It was a cold afternoon in late December as I sat at my desk quietly reflecting on my first few months as the supervisor of the "shock troops." Indeed, it had been going well. Then my phone rang, and when I picked it up, I heard the hushed voice of Jack, one of my subordinates. He said I should come to the underground parking garage right away. He wouldn't say why, but he spoke with some urgency.

Curious, I hurried to the garage and met Jack at the designated location. He introduced me to Ralph and Vinnie, who were standing alongside an old gray sedan, obviously weighted down in the back. I had never met them before, but I recognized the name of their roofing firm as one that had won a number of our construction projects.

As they looked around the garage and talked in hushed tones, they moved to open the trunk of the old car as I looked on in trepidation. What was this all about? Was there a body in there? Much to my relief, there wasn't.

But somewhat to my disbelief, it contained cases of liquor, all of the top brands. "Here, help yourself. Pick out a little something for your family," Ralph whispered. Seeing the look of bewilderment on my face, he said, "This is just a little Christmas gift from us to say thank you for being such a good customer."

Put on the spot, I wasn't sure what to do. I remembered in years past, the conference table in the state architect's office filled with such bottles at the holidays. I thought of the similar bottle given to my electrician father by the supplier who was thankful for his business. I made a mental note that all of the projects this firm was doing for us were awarded through an open, competitive bidding process. And I thought of the Public Officers Law that allowed a gift of up to seventy-five dollars in a given year. I didn't want to appear rude or ungrateful, so I decided to graciously accept one bottle. After all, it was acceptable by both custom and the prevailing rules of the day.

On reflection, this is a case of where I learned by doing something wrong. In spite of the rationale I developed in the pressure of the moment, after having time to think about it, I decided that accepting such a gift was wrong. Even though it did not break the letter of the law or any organizational policies at the time, it would clearly give the appearance of a conflict of interest. While the individual contracts themselves were competitively bid, my staff would be involved in inspections, quality control, and approval of materials. Even more significantly, the negotiation of change orders required judgment and presented significant latitude. There was, indeed, room for actual conflict.

I did not view this incident as any effort to bribe a public official, just a common courtesy in the construction industry at the time. Further, I never suspected any wrongdoing on the part of my staff or anything other than a full-out effort to enforce our contracts and protect the State. Believe me, I monitored their work very closely.

But times have changed, and the standards and customs of those days, which allowed for such activity, are largely a thing of the past. While state and local laws may still allow the acceptance of small gifts, many public-sector organizations have promulgated either formal or informal policies or ethics guidelines that reflect the public expectation for perfection and high standards of integrity from our public servants. Such standards prohibit gifts of any kind whatsoever, especially for people in policy-making positions. Clearly, there cannot be any real or perceived conflict of interest in the execution of the public's work, and public employees must not benefit personally by way of their official position, whether it's a bottle of liquor or tickets to a ball game.

To achieve credibility as a transformational public leader, you must set the integrity bar high and follow the practice of accepting nothing of any kind, whether or not your laws or agency guidelines permit it. Your integrity must be unquestioned! Your staff must see that you are unwavering in this regard and that you will neither tolerate nor ignore those who are not. Your staff needs to see that you neither seek nor receive any special benefit because of your position. Expect and demand the same from every person in your organization.

Now, this doesn't sound like rocket science, does it? But I could fill a bucket with the stupidity of people I have known who have let their position, power, or greed guide them into doing inappropriate things, things well beyond taking a free lunch or bottle of wine. I don't have enough fingers to count those I have known who have actually gone to jail or lost their jobs because they lacked the integrity needed to lead.

Kickbacks, bribery, extortion, nepotism, free vacations, sex—just a sample of the misdeeds. You can do an internet search on some of the political luminaries in New York, where I come from, and read the scandalous details for yourself. Just in the relatively recent past, the careers of the elected leaders in both houses of the legislature, as well as the governor, were derailed by such lack of integrity. A while before that, the state comptroller was defrocked for equally poor decisions. Easier yet, open the paper any day of the week in any town in America and you will probably find someone in the public sector being accused of doing something wrong.

On the staff level, I've seen an agency commissioner send civil servants to run personal errands. I've seen leasing agents take bribes to steer contracts in a certain direction. I've seen alcoholism, sexual harassment, insurance fraud, misuse of public property, voter fraud, extramarital affairs between married coworkers, poor attendance, conflicts with private business ventures, concert tickets, lavish dinners, and a host of other transgressions that totally destroyed whatever credibility that leader may have had.

I am writing this book in the sincere hope that you and your contemporaries can help reform and reinvent our public entities through transformational change. But this can be accomplished only by credible leaders who exhibit unquestioned integrity. Doing the kinds of stupid things mentioned above will serve only to destroy the credibility of the leader and perpetuate the deterioration of our public institutions and public confidence in them. If our public organizations are left to languish because of a lack of credible leadership, our very society and way of life are threatened.

Being a transformational public leader is challenge enough, and one does not need to have a promising career derailed for a relatively insignificant benefit. As the transformation of your organization evolves, it must be a model of doing it right in every respect. Your integrity and that of your organization must be beyond question. Again, integrity is a critical component of your credibility, and you can't allow the Ralphs and Vinnies of the world to mess it up! As I tell my kids all the time, don't do anything stupid!

Chapter 38

Back at the Dinner Table

Remember that tiny little dinner table in chapter 8? Reflecting back on it, I think there were many more lessons passed on at that table than I knew or understood at the time. My father was a man of few words and tended to speak in sound bites. And while some of those sound bites may have been cliché, they left a powerful impression on me as a young kid. Some lasted a lifetime.

One of the most memorable is when he advised, "Honesty is the best policy!" I suspect this particular dinner table topic was triggered by some transgression where I was less than forthcoming with the entirety of truth. I can't remember for sure, but it may have been when my friend and I helped ourselves to a snack of scallions from our neighbor's garden and then tried to claim that we hadn't done it. Breath mint, anyone?

Our own kids were known to tell a fib or two, like the time they came home from school and announced the results of the annual fire-prevention poster contest. Our daughter blasted through the door brandishing a shiny bronze trophy, which had been

Out of the Clay

awarded in recognition of her first-place win in the kindergarten. Following closely behind her was our second-grader son, who was clutching a red second-place ribbon. As we fawned and fussed over both of them, our son quickly explained that he too had won first place but lamented that "they were all out of first-place trophies!" Kid stuff! All normal and expected. Just teaching opportunities. (BTW, we have never let him forget this one!)

But when the practice of little childhood fibs carries over into adult life, trouble ensues. The leader, especially, cannot resort to "kid stuff," as honesty is one of the most critical dimensions of credibility. Honesty is not just the best policy. For the transformational leader, it is the ONLY policy!

This is different than the topic of integrity that I discussed in the last chapter. That was all about those things that are illegal, unethical, or immoral, things that can send you to jail or into unemployment or early retirement. Such things can ruin a career or, at best, derail any effort at transformation.

This chapter is simply about telling the truth, all the time in every circumstance. Unless you can establish a clear, unequivocal reputation for being honest, you will not have credibility as a leader! Lack of this kind of honesty will not send you to jail, but it will, without a doubt, block any effort at effective transformation or organizational reinvention. From your subordinates' point of view, if you cannot be trusted, you cannot be followed.

Seems pretty simple, doesn't it? I found it one of the easiest rules to follow throughout my career as I have heard my father's words echo time and time again. Honesty is the best policy, and your people can tell if you are truthful with them. As a wonderful byproduct of honesty, you never have to untangle your lies or remember what stories you told to whom and when. You never have to find your way out of a tangled web.

There are a number of dimensions to this honesty thing. I have seen cases where the leader promises something to a subordinate in return for extra work, a special assignment or something else, but then doesn't follow through. Leaders who promise things they cannot deliver quickly lose credibility. Sadly, sometimes there was no intention to deliver in the first place.

Another form of dishonesty is being inconsistent in the expression of values and actual practice. I once had a supervisor who was coaching me by telling me, "The leader has to take fear out of the equation." He must have just read that in a book or something because I saw this same person threaten to throw someone "out the window and hold him by his ankles" until he promised to plead guilty to some infraction. On another occasion, he wanted to punish me because of something one of my people did that, although consistent with agency policy, he didn't like. But he lamented his fate by telling me, "I guess you're going to skate on this because you were on vacation when it happened!" Oh sure, no fear there.

Another common variance with stated values is where the leader professes an allegiance to "family first" or work/life balance and then works people to death. I once saw an agency commissioner who called staff meetings at 5:00 or 6:00 p.m., including Fridays. Another leader was described to me as "She consumes her people." I've seen vacations denied and parents with sick kids shown no flexibility or compassion whatsoever. So much for family first.

Then there is the gossiper, you know, the person who knows everything about everybody and can't wait to tell you all they know. There is nothing really so confidential that he can't share with at least someone. If you see or hear this kind of behavior from your leader, watch out.

Remember Lu Baker and her list of Irish and homegrown sayings? She often used a timeworn phrase that applies here: "If a dog will bring you a bone, he'll carry one." I learned the hard way that if a person is sharing juicy tidbits about others with you, he's sharing things he knows about you with someone else. Gossip is a form of dishonesty that will certainly erode your credibility as a leader and do nothing but demonstrate a lack of respect for those in your charge.

Out of the Clay

I'm sure you have heard the expression "talk the talk." It refers to the person who has read the literature, attended the seminars, and become expert on a topic that they discuss ad nauseam—but then nothing happens. For the leader to have credibility, it is critically necessary to "walk the talk," or do what you say you are going to do. You have to put your words into practice and deliver.

Take, for example, the school principal who promises to be there when one of his teachers has to meet with a set of irate parents regarding the suspension of their son from school. The teacher has had trouble with these parents in the past and, quite frankly, is intimidated. Support of the principal is critical.

Then the day comes and the teacher and parents are assembled, but no principal. Multiple attempts to get him on the phone go unanswered and his secretary eventually informs the teacher she will have to handle this herself. Apparently, he was in his office with the door locked and would not respond. No jail time for this dishonesty, but no credibility either!

Remember the knucklehead in chapter 10 who held the crumpled paper under the table with the names of Alice and Mildred—and then pretended to express concern or interest in their well-being? Not honest! Not credible! This executive would have been much more honest and credible if he said, "I'm sorry. I don't remember the names of your daughters but wanted to ask how they are doing." A single incident is not a big deal, but such a pattern of behavior can destroy credibility.

Honesty sometimes demands courage. I once worked for a commissioner who was one of the smartest executives I ever met. But he was never afraid to say that he didn't understand something, even more than once. He was always sincere and honest, and for that we believed in his credibility.

I once had a Machiavellian-style boss who became "animated" (as he would say) and royally bawled out the entire executive team for something that happened on a project. Over time, the estimated cost had grown to be well over the budget, mostly because of upgrades he had added himself. He advised that we were getting paid to advise him in order to avoid such situations, and if we couldn't do that, somebody was going to get fired.

A bit later, I convened the entire team and developed a consensus solution to another significant technical problem. When I presented our recommendation to the boss, he just waived me off without dialogue or comment. Somewhat annoyed, I reminded him that he had demanded we give him solid advice. To that he responded, "It doesn't mean I have to take it," and walked away. Credible leader? Certainly not!

And one of my favorite stories is of an executive who headed a good-sized public organization that was housed in a large building. Around Christmas, staff placed a bin in the main lobby of the building where donations of food for needy families could be placed. An additional bin was placed inside the executive suite on the top floor where those who were a bit better off could make their own contributions.

Suspicions developed that this chief executive was taking items out of the lobby bin and placing them in the executive bin, thereby passing them off as his own personal donations. Early one morning, an enterprising staff member marked two boxes of spaghetti and placed them in an easy-to-grab location in the lobby bin. Guess what turned up in the executive bin later that morning? Busted! Honest leader? Don't think so!

This is one of the simplest and easiest-to-understand concepts presented in this book. Honesty in every respect, in every form, in every circumstance, in every interaction, all the time is the only policy. Without it, the leader cannot establish credibility and cannot lead a transformation.

CHAPTER 39

MULTIPLE CHOICE

Remember those multiple-choice tests we used to have in school? I loved those because you knew the right answer was there someplace. But when "all of the above" was an option, it complicated things, especially if you were already debating between two answers that looked credible. Maybe they were all correct, but you couldn't always be sure!

Well, at this point in the book, "all of the above" is the correct answer. While I have just explored many of the specific dimensions of credibility, such as honesty, integrity, energy, optimism, presence, and credentials, virtually everything discussed in the preceding four parts of the book contributes to credibility.

First of all, in the discussion of respect, and the ability to garner it, the attributes of honesty, sincerity, humility, and compassion are all addressed in a variety of ways, all of which contribute to the credibility of the leader. This theme of respect suggests that leadership is not about the leader, but about the followers.

A leader who shows respect for the followers and puts them

first is truly credible. The leader who gives all the credit for accomplishments to the people in the organization, but takes personal responsibility for failure, is far more believable than one who hogs the credit for success while assessing blame when success is not achieved.

Credibility is further fueled by the leader's undeniable effort to find and capture the individual and collective self-esteem of the organization, the holy grail of transformational leadership. Leaders who refuse to feed their own egos at the expense of others are truly believable.

Followers expect their leaders to be forward looking, and that's what our discussion of vision was all about. It's more than just having some idea on where to go. Workers can take care of the day-to-day mechanics of any operation, but they expect the leader to articulate the possibilities of what tomorrow can bring. A leader without vision is a leader in name only.

And then there was our discussion of courage. Leaders who are timid are just not believable. As we discussed, there are many difficult things a leader must do, challenges that must be faced, and hard decisions to be made. In spite of having respect, vision, and many other positive attributes, a leader who cannot, or will not, face up to and take on these difficult responsibilities lacks sufficient credibility to lead a transformation.

Finally, to be truly believable, a leader needs to exhibit the power of intuition and the willingness to use it. To my way of thinking, a total and unquestioned reliance on numbers isn't a lot different than referring everything to a committee and doing whatever the committee recommends. Both are an abdication of the leader's responsibility to lead. When the leader supplements the analytical process with this power or sense of what is right, credibility is enhanced.

So, in the end, there are many factors that contribute to a leader's credibility. And the closer you come to exhibiting all of the above attributes, the greater will be your credibility as a leader.

PART VII

FINAL THOUGHTS

Chapter 40

The Pond

I'm not sure where my love of loud, bold marching music began. It could very well have been when I was about six years old and my father took me to a parade one night in old downtown Troy, New York. I can remember vividly the black uniforms, the upbeat cadence, the blaring brass, and the thunderous drums of the newly formed Empire State Grenadiers drum and bugle corps, the highlight of the night. Yes, that must have been it!

From that moment on, I wanted nothing more than to play my horn. Following that first little performance for my grandmother, all the way through college and beyond, I took every opportunity I could to wail on that trumpet: concert band, jazz band, wind ensemble, marching bands, dance bands, and drum corps.

All of this experience paid off during my junior year in college. I knew I would be attending ROTC summer camp when the academic year was over, and I saw an opportunity to hone my drill-instructor skills. The local volunteer fire department had a little

Out of the Clay

marching band of young people that provided music for parade appearances, and I volunteered to lead it.

When I showed up, I found a pretty ragtag bunch of kids dressed in blue shorts, knee socks, and berets who were trying to play music that was too complicated. They were embarrassed to appear in public, and the cacophony of sounds they were making was hard on the ears. This group was clearly in need of a makeover.

The transformation happened quickly, however. New drum corps–style uniforms with military shako hats and plumes, more and better instruments, and some easy-to-play, great-sounding music. This new music included a very simple fanfare I arranged myself. In writing it, I used only two notes for each of the "voices" in an effort to give them early success and show them just how easy it was to make a big, beautiful sound.

It was very rewarding to watch as this ever-growing group of young people came together to learn, to bond, and to work as a team. Some of them had had nothing to do before getting involved with this endeavor, and most of them had no experience with music. In many cases, we just put a bugle or set of drumsticks in their hands, gave them some basic instruction, and turned them loose.

Their pride in what they were doing was palpable, and it was reflected in growing community interest and support. Increasing numbers of young people came by and asked to join, all wanting to be part of this exciting venture.

The group quickly outgrew my ability to teach them the music side of it, and we had to bring in professional instructors, who took them to the next level. What began as strictly a parade group soon moved up to field competition. During their successful run as the Killmen Junior Drum and Bugle Corps, they put small-town Wynantskill, New York, on the map.

But eventually the time came when I had to show up for life and leave the group behind. But the memories of those kids would endure! Okay, so what's the point? Where's the leadership lesson here? Please read on.

Part VII: Final Thoughts — The Pond

One Saturday morning a while back, I woke to find an email that had been sent to me very late the night before. Even though I had not seen or heard from him in almost fifty years, I immediately recognized the author as one of those young kids who participated in that drum and bugle corps so many years before.

It began, "You probably don't remember me, but with a two-note fanfare, you changed my life." What?! That blew me away!

The message went on to say, "You know when you drop a stone into a pond how it produces a series of rings ... well that's exactly what happened with our little hometown [drum] corps. ... Do you understand what an influence you had on the lives of the original members of the Killmen? The whole experience blossomed out from having a small performance ensemble for firemen to march down the street to an organization that created an appreciation for music, a knowledge of teamwork, and lifelong friendships. What a gift! ... Bill, I just wanted to thank you for doing this forty-nine years ago."

In his message, Jay McBride explained how this experience had such a profound and lasting influence on the lives of so many of those kids involved. He explained, "Although it only lasted for six years, it gave a place for young people to learn, grow, and socialize. It was also a breeding ground for talented people who became performers, designers, and instructors in the activity on a national level and beyond."

Then Jay listed at least a dozen well-known national drum corps and musical organizations where his friends from back then became involved, some as music arrangers, while others were performers or instructors. One of the youngest kids even became a trombonist with the Boston Symphony, while Jay himself studied with the Syracuse Symphony Orchestra. He still writes music for brass ensembles, and when I'm lucky, he shares his works in progress with me.

This story reflects a very simple but profound message. Transformational leaders have impacts that go well beyond the immediacy of the organization—its processes, its people, and its performance. When I handed eight-year-old Sean Baker that one-valve bugle in 1964, did I have any notion that one day he would perform with the Boston Symphony? When I was teaching Jay McBride that very simple two-note fanfare, could I possibly envision that he would be writing beautiful music and teaching brass some fifty years later?

The impacts of the true leader transcend the business of the day and, like ripples from that stone dropped in the pond, touch untold shores in unforeseen ways. I often think of those who dropped stones in the pond for me and wish they could see what their work produced. I wish Jean Tracy could have seen me speaking to two thousand people in a packed convention center. I wish Gene Halsey could have witnessed the radical transformation of the organization that I led only twenty years after he recommended me for promotion. And if John Egan could have only seen me out in the dark night, with the mud, the water, and the flashing lights, supporting and encouraging the men and women at the "end of the system," he would rest in the certain knowledge that his legacy endures.

Stone after stone, ripple after ripple, life becomes a pattern of intersecting waves that come together in forms and shapes we cannot predict! While Jean Tracy and Gene Halsey and John Egan, and so very many others, are no longer with us, the lessons they taught and examples they set are carried with me to this day. Every stone I drop in the pond myself transmits the influence of those who have come before me to events, organizations, and people well beyond anything they could ever know or imagine.

If you are the powerful transformational leader I hope you will become, you will have touched their hearts and minds and ignited a passion within your people that will stick with them for a lifetime. Such passion will lead to untold acts of accomplishment and contribution. Every great thing they do, every life they touch in a positive way, every contribution they make, this all becomes part of your own legacy.

Part VII: Final Thoughts   The Pond

    I shared with you in the beginning that I think I could have done much better if I had this little book when I started my career. You see, I went through all those years blindly unaware of the powerful influence I was having on people and events as yet unknown. And it wasn't until I received this little out-of-the-blue message from Jay McBride that I came to more fully understand that the leader's impact and influence live well beyond the immediacy of that moment in time, beyond that initial splash in the water. It is clear to me now that the ripples radiate long after the stone has settled out of sight.

    So, as you answer your calling to become part of a new generation of passionate public leaders, righting the ship of state one office, one bureau, one division, or one department at a time, think beyond the limits of today to the example you are setting, the messages you are sending, and the impact all of this can have on people and events yet unknown. Rest with the certain knowledge that your legacy will endure!

Chapter 41

The Tree

My final story is set on a quiet stretch of lane, just around the corner from that tiny house where I grew up. An abandoned section of the old Winter Street Extension, this unpaved strip wasn't much longer than a football field and was lined with beautiful maple trees.

Often, on hot summer days, I would take shelter in the cool shade of one of those big old trees and just sit there, thinking. I'd think about what life had been like so far and I'd think about what the future might hold. What would my story be? What kind of person might I become? I have to admit that, even in those early years, I sensed that I wanted to be leading somebody or something somewhere.

Earlier on, I asked you to reflect on your own story as you learned about mine. I asked you to contemplate what you might do and who you might be. In this age of incredible speed of information flow and powerful technology, it has become convenient to ask Alexa, Siri, Nina, or some other "intelligent voice assistant" for help. But they can't answer everything—not yet. Once in a while, there is no substitute for the human mind and its ability to contemplate and envision some future state.

So I ask you now to find a quiet place where you can think for a while. A place where you can reflect upon what you have read and how this favorite quote of mine might translate for you, what it might mean in the context of your life:

> *Success is not something that can measured or worn on a watch or hung on the wall. It is not the esteem of colleagues, or the admiration of the community, or the appreciation of patients. Success is the certain knowledge that you have become yourself, the person you were meant to be from all time.*
>
> —Dr. George A. Sheehan
> Physician, Runner, Author, Motivational Speaker

As I sit here writing in my favorite little coffee shop in Milton, Georgia, some thousand miles from that big old maple, I continue to contemplate the future. But now, it's not about me. It's about you.

I wonder about who you were meant to be and what you were born to do. What will success look like for you? Will it be as one of those passionate public leaders we have been talking about, the brand of leader that our country, our communities, and our society so desperately need? Is that how you will make a difference and give purpose and meaning to your life and the lives of others? I certainly hope so!

Looking back now, I see life as a set of loosely connected moments in time where, every once in a while, the stars are perfectly aligned. It is during these brief moments that you must seize the opportunity to make your difference and become that person you were meant to be!

Acknowledgments

I want to first thank my family. My wife, Anne, has patiently reviewed every chapter of this book more than once and provided me with invaluable insights and perspectives. And then our children, William, Christine, and Gregory, whose life experiences provided fodder for some of my stories and inspiration for others. Additionally, their chapter reviews and feedback were most helpful. I want to thank my sister, Carol Burke, for filling in some of the details of our family history and for her willingness to allow me to tell the world that she didn't eat her brussels sprouts.

I owe Ron Wallace a debt of gratitude for providing such a wonderful foreword for my work. Given his singular standing as a global leader, it is indeed an honor for me to have had him share his thoughts in this manner.

To Robert Eccleston, I owe thanks for allowing me to share the story of his life and his work. This, indeed, inspired the concept for this book. And to Jay McBride, for reaching out to me after some fifty years since I had last seen him to tell me of the impact I had on him and a group of other young people.

There were a number of people who assisted me with filling in

Out of the Clay

the blanks and getting the facts right for the stories about Joe Bulmer, John Egan, and Jack Thero. Lucie Marion, Paul Bulmer, John O'Donnell, Cathy Nicolas, Tina Anthony, and Patty Bligh all provided me with important information and insights. Then John Egan and Jack Thero both personally reviewed my draft and offered some key clarifications.

I owe Ilene Hinchey a debt of gratitude for her review of the chapter that features her husband, Maurice, and the Catskills Interpretive Center, and Sue Halsey Westphal for sharing information about her father, Eugene Halsey. I also want to thank Clarence Stukes for teaching me about the power of diversity. It was this understanding that inspired me to share my own story.

And then there are my colleagues from New York State and Arlington, Virginia, who allowed me to tell you about them. Dave Seiffert, Jim Dirolf, Mike Singleton, Doris Jackson, Inta Malis, Jim Jamieson, Diane McGuirk, Jim Davies, and Bob Palmer all made chapter reviews and helped me keep the facts straight.

I was fortunate enough to have several young colleagues who were willing to review early drafts of many of the chapters to see if I was getting started in the right direction. Angela Thompson, Tamara Galliani, and Bethany Usry all provided valuable insights and suggestions.

And finally, this book would not have been possible without the superbly professional and talented team at my publisher, BookLogix.

About the Author

The son of working-class parents, William F. O'Connor III was born and raised in a small rural town in Upstate New York. He graduated from Columbia High School in East Greenbush, New York, and went on to Rensselaer Polytechnic Institute in Troy, New York, where he earned bachelor's and master's degrees in the building sciences, architecture, and business administration.

After attaining a license to practice architecture, his professional career took an unexpected turn when he discovered a passion for public leadership. Having had a childhood dream of designing beautiful buildings, he was initially disappointed and frustrated when the only opportunity that presented itself upon graduation was in the public sector. But it didn't take long for him to realize that public service is an honorable profession and that public leadership is, indeed, a high calling. And so, the dream of building buildings was quickly supplanted by the passionate desire to lead people and make a significant difference in their lives and in the lives of those served.

Over more than forty-five years of public service, O'Connor led transformative change in almost every position he held, from first-line supervisor on up. As deputy commissioner in the New York State Office of General Services, he orchestrated what was literally a worst-to-first reinvention of the billion-dollar design and construction program. Later, in Arlington County, Virginia, he was instrumental in advancing a number of major initiatives, including the total reorganization of the Department of Environmental Services.

O'Connor's passion for leadership also showed itself in a meaningful record of community service as member or chair of almost a dozen boards and organizations. Most notable among these were his record of accomplishment as chairman of the Board of Trustees at Hudson Valley Community College in Troy, New York, and his distinguished eighteen years of leadership of the Board of Education in the Averill Park Central School District. All of this sharpened his understanding of public leadership and the key personal qualities that are required for transformational change.

A Vietnam veteran, O'Connor was a captain in the US Army Corps of Engineers. He was awarded both the Army Commendation Medal and the Bronze Star for meritorious service. An avid runner, he has completed seven marathons and numerous half marathons and 10K races. In addition to writing, he spends time as an abstract painter.

He currently lives in Milton, Georgia, with his wife, Anne. The couple has three grown children and ten grandchildren.